THE
BOSTON
RED SOX

THE
BOSTON
RED SOX

AN ILLUSTRATED HISTORY

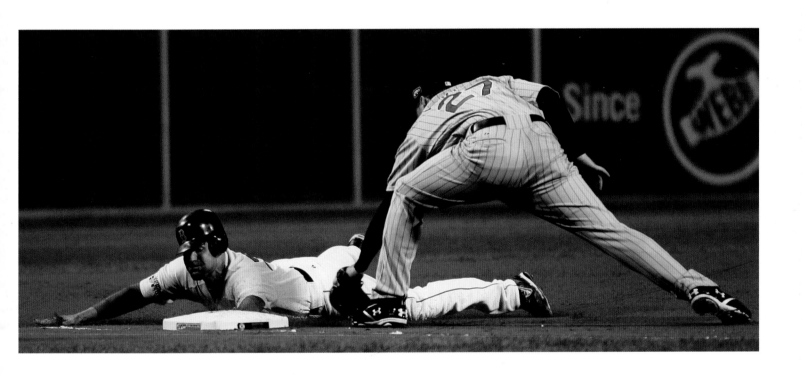

Milton Cole & Jim Kaplan
Foreword by Johnny Pesky

JG
PRESS

Page 1: *The Colorado Rockies and the Boston Red Sox line up for the National Anthem before the start of Game 1 of the 2007 World Series at Fenway Park on October 24, 2007, in Boston.*

Page 2: *Red Sox starter Josh Beckett winds up in Game 1 of the 2007 World Series, which Boston won 13-1.*

Page 3: *Mike Lowell slides safely under the tag of Colorado Rockies third baseman Garrett Atkins in Game 2 of the 2007 World Series.*

This Page: *Ted Williams hits a long ball in September 1958, the year he won his sixth and final batting title.*

PICTURE CREDITS

AP Photo/Elise Amendola: 7 (top), 88 (bottom).
AP Photo/Charles Rex Arbogast: 89 (left).
AP Photo/Al Behrman: 90.
AP Photo/Duane Burleson: 89 (right).
AP Photo/Gail Burton: 86 (right).
AP Photo/Kevork Djansezian: 88 (top).
AP Photo/Mark Humphrey: 91, 93.
AP Photo/Linda Kaye: 79.
AP Photo/Bill Kostroun: 7 (bottom), 85.
AP Photo/Charles Krupa: 8 (bottom), 80 (right), 81, 87 (left).
AP Photo/Mark Lennihan: 83.
AP Photo/William B. Plowman: 84.
AP Photo/Lisa Poole: 92.
AP Photo/Jim Rogash: 78, 82.
AP Photo/Steven Senne: 80 (left).
AP Photo/Chitose Suzuki: 86 (left).
AP Photo/Winslow Townson: 87 (right).
Bettmann Archive: 9 (bottom), 17 (bottom right).
Mike Blake/Reuters/Corbis: 94 (bottom).
Malcolm Emmons: 41, 43 (left), 45.
Getty Images: 2, 3, 97 (top), 98, 99, 100 (both), 101 (both), 102 (both), 103 (both), 104 (both), 105 (both), 106 (both), 107 (top), 108 (both), 109 (both).
Nancy Hogue: 46 (both), 47, 49, 53, 54, 55 (both), 56-57, 58 (both), 59 (both), 61(bottom).
Icon SMI/Corbis: 95 (top and bottom).
MLB/Getty Images: 1, 6 (bottom), 107 (bottom).
Ron Modra: 69.
National Baseball Library, Cooperstown, NY: 6 (top left), 10-11, 12 (both), 14, 15, 16 (top), 19, 21, 23 (top), 25 (top), 32, 35 (left), 42.
Ponzini Photography: 60, 61 (top), 62, 63 (bottom), 64, 65 (both), 66 (top), 67 (top), 68, 70, 71 (both), 72 (both), 73, 74 (both), 75 (both), 76, 77.
Samantha Press: 9 (bottom).
Jessica Rinaldi/Reuters/Corbis: 97 (bottom).
Brian Snyder/Reuters/Corbis: 94 (top), 96.
UPI/Bettmann Newsphotos: 4-5, 9 (top), 13, 17 (top, bottom left), 18, 20, 22, 23 (bottom), 24, 25 (bottom), 26, 27 (both), 28, 29, 30, 31, 33 (both), 35 (both), 36, 37, 38-39, 40, 43 (bottom right), 44, 48, 50, 51 (both), 52, 63 (top), 66 (bottom), 67 (bottom).
Endpaper photo courtesy of Boston Red Sox.

ACKNOWLEDGMENTS

The publisher would like to thank the following people who helped in the preparation of this book: John Kirk, Barbara Thrasher, John S. Bowman and Emily Zelner, who edited it; Doron "Duke" Goldman, for his sharp fact-checking; Don Longabucco, who designed it; Rita Longabucco, who did the picture research; Greg Scott, who wrote the captions; and Elizabeth McCarthy, who prepared the index.

Published by World Publications Group, Inc.
140 Laurel Street
East Bridgewater, MA 02333
www.wrldpub.net

Copyright ©2009 World Publications Group, Inc.

ISBN 1-57215-523-X
978-1-57215-523-7

Printed and bound in China by SNP Leefung Printers Limited.

1 2 3 4 5 06 05 03 02

Contents

Foreword

Above: *A Boston Rooters pin from 1897. The avid Royal Rooters fans cheered on the National League Boston Beaneaters, but when the upstart American League Boston team came to town in 1901, the Rooters' expansive enthusiasm encompassed them as well.*

Below: *A Red Sox player-manager-instructor since 1940, Johnny Pesky throws out the ceremonial first pitch of Game 2 of the 2004 World Series. In September 2008 the Red Sox retired Pesky's number 6.*

Johnny Pesky wrote this after the Sox won the World Series in 2004, but his words are at least as appropriate now that he has witnessed yet another championship.

You always remember your first home run. You're so tickled about it, but winning the World Series? That's another thing completely.

I've been waiting more than sixty years for this. I joined the Red Sox organization in 1940. I can remember the 1946 World Series; the two best hitters had bad Series — Williams and Musial. I thought '48, '49, '50, we had as good a team as you could put on the field. Something always seemed to happen. We thought there was a black cat on the squad or something.

In 1986, I was sitting with Mele and Malzone, and I said, "We got 'em now." I opened my mouth too soon. The ball went through poor Buckner's legs. I really felt bad for him. I had a good feeling in 2003, but it didn't work out. We've been so close so many times and got aced out so many times.

This took the sting out of a lot of all the bad feelings of years back — personal feelings and stuff like that. Winning the World Series takes care of a multitude of sins. It was so heart-warming. I saw men cry tears of joy, and I was as bad as anybody. Wakefield gave me the trophy to hold. Some of them were a little happy for my sake. Some of them who have been around me long enough know what this meant to someone like me. "This is for you, Johnny"— Schilling said it, and so did Derek Lowe. I guess it took me over a week to come down out of the clouds.

When we were three down to the Yankees, I said, "Oh, my God." I think someone must have shined a star on this team.

I got doused by champagne. All over. I had a raincoat on. It's a good thing I did because, Jesus, I really got drenched.

When this happens to you late in your life, it makes you feel good, like you've turned the full cycle. You've played. You've messed up. You got a hit. You may have won a ballgame with a base on balls or a base hit or a fly ball. When you're around the game your whole life — and I've been very fortunate to spend most of my life with the Boston Red Sox....

I looked up in the heavens and I thought of Mr. Yawkey. And Cronin. Eddie Collins. Ted was the first one I thought of. I thought about Ted and I thought about Dom and I thought about Bobby. A Rhodes Scholar I'm not, but I thought about the people who were here when we were young guys. Vern Stephens, Dropo, Tom McBride, George Metkovich, Birdie Tebbetts. And I heard from people I hadn't heard from for years. You should have seen the mail. Every damn day, my mail...

Most of all I thought of the loyal fans — I'm happy for the people who went to the ballpark day in and day out, year in and year out. For this to happen — and the way it happened, being down three games to the Yankees and then beat them four in a row. And then beat the Cardinals.

I shed a few happy tears and I'm unashamed of it. We felt like a bunch of children, just so elated with such a good feeling. You've been around here all these years, and you see fans pouring into that ballpark all these years, and rooting so hard for you to get a base hit or strike out the opposition. I'm glad we won, because of the fans. I've been in the game my whole life, and never won a World Series. When this happens to you, you're completely in seventh heaven.

— Johnny Pesky
January 2005

Above: *In Game 2 of the 2004 World Series against the St. Louis Cardinals, Red Sox third baseman Bill Mueller caught this line drive, then turned a double play by tagging Cardinal Reggie Sanders out at third.*

Left: *Johnny Damon, a favorite of Red Sox fans with his long hair and uninhibited manner, here hits one of his two homers that helped to defeat the Yankees in the 7th game and clinch the 2004 American League Championship. Looking on are Yankee catcher Jorge Posada and umpire Randy Marsh.*

It's About Us

I wrote the following tribute to the Red Sox, baseball and the fans after the incredible triumphs of 2004 and now all of us have lived to see the Sox win another Series championship. Although nothing can ever replace the experience and feelings inspired by that 2004 season, I feel that the 2007 season has only magnified and validated the sentiments expressed here.

It's the history of the Red Sox, but it's really the history of us. Uncle Leo was born in 1918 — the same week as Ted Williams. He's been waiting for 86 years.

Addicted and proud of it, we all love the Red Sox. We love the logo. We love Fenway. We love the Nation.

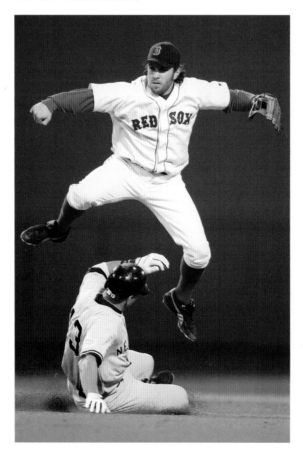

My father brought his eight-year-old from the dark beneath the city streets to the heavenly promise of Fenway. I did the same with Samantha, Melissa and Michael. We went for the potential, the beauty, the pleasure. We went for everything except the success — until this year.

The Red Sox teach us history, teach us life; the Red Sox keep us all connected.

What if...
If we've learned anything from the Red Sox, we've learned "nothing is easy." Shoulda, coulda, woulda is our mantra. "What if" is the Red Sox story, our story. This one time — 2004 — the "what ifs" went our way…

What if one inch lower for Tony Clark — the ball hits the wall? He joins Boone, Buckner, Bucky and Babe as a legendary tormentor. But it's one inch higher for a meaningless ground rule double.

What if we bench a slumping Damon for Game 7: Damon's first six games: 3 Hits, 0 RBIs. Damon's Game 7: First three innings: 3 Hits, 6 RBIs.

What if the umpire rules for A-Rod and his slap? This joins Ed Armbrister and Carlton Fisk among the many mistaken calls in Red Sox history? This time, however, the umpire gets it right.

What if Bellhorn's winning homerun doesn't hit the Pesky Pole?

What if we don't give the much beleaguered Derek Lowe a shot — and he doesn't clinch the last game of each playoff series?

What if we don't give Schilling and his bloody ankle the ball?

What if there was no David Ortiz?

In baseball, as in life, it's always "what if." Both are games of inches. This way or that — a thin line separating love and hate, triumph and tragedy.

What if we go one for four? Ordinary.
What if we go one for three?

Extraordinary.

What if we finally win eight in a row—after losing the first three? **Miraculous!**

Game 7. Aunt Muriel says it was 6-3, 7-3, 10-3. Still "those bums are going to blow it." She goes upstairs. Later she hears Uncle Leo screaming, shrieking. "Either he was dying or the Red Sox…*won?!*"

It's Not About Baseball—
It's About Us

It's not about Pedro and Varitek and Terry. We were here long before those guys and we'll be here long after them. Our first name is "long-suffering." It means a lot to the players but it means so much more to us.

It's about Melissa. She couldn't take much more. She shut her eyes hoping for the last out. Then the most beautiful anthem ever—"Dirty Water" began to play. It's over. Everything will be ok.

It's about Michael. Game 5. Five hours and forty-nine minutes, 14 innings—the longest post-season game in history. Ortiz wins it again. His third walk-off hit in the post-season! At long last we start to leave—well after the game ends. But no one is in the aisles. No one is leaving. We stand alone in a full stadium.

"Dad, was this the best game in Red Sox history?" Michael asks his father, who was at the Carlton Fisk Game 6 of 1975. His father

is still thinking about that one.

It's about Samantha who answers her own question as the World Series ends: What does it all mean? "Life as we know it will never be the same."

It's about fate.

It's about a lunar eclipse when a guy named Luna comes to bat.

It's about a Cardinal with Babe's number 3 making the last out of the series.

It's about Manny exclaiming, "We're a team of destination."

It's not about baseball. It's about justice, redemption, heroism, pride and respect. Thank you Red Sox of 1946, 1967, 1975, 1986, but the 2004 team was the greatest team in Red Sox history. There will never be another event like the 2004 Red Sox.

—Jeff Press, CEO
JG Press Publishing
(Lifelong Red Sox fan)

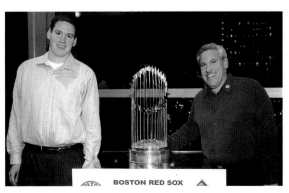

Above: *The Red Sox pitching staff poses the day before their team takes on the Phillies in the 1915 World Series, which Boston won, four games to one. Pictured from left to right: Rube Foster, Carl Mays, Ernie Shore, Babe Ruth and Dutch Leonard.*

Below: *It's about us—happy at last!*

1. Off and Running

Boston has always been a baseball town. By at least the 1850s it was supporting numerous amateur teams. And when America's professional ball clubs, concentrated in the Northeast, formed their first organization in 1871, the National Association of Professional Base Ball Players, the Red Stockings of Cincinnati moved to Boston and soon were the scourge of professional baseball, winning four straight Association championships from 1872-75. It was this Boston team that, with the Philadelphia Athletics, went off to England in 1874 and played a series of exhibition games there – both cricket and baseball.

William Hulbert, president of the Chicago White Stockings, was jealous of the success of this Boston team, and in 1875 he secretly bought four of the stars – Albert Spalding, Roscoe Barnes, Cal McVey and "Deacon" Jim White. Boston and the other teams were so furious that they threatened to expel Chicago from the National Association. Hulbert outflanked them, though, by proposing that all the teams agree on such matters as the hiring of players; out of this came, in February 1876, the formation of the National League of Professional Base Ball Clubs. Boston at once fell to third place in that 1876 season, but it regained first place in 1877 and 1878. This Boston National team continued to give the local fans much to cheer about, but Boston was clearly ready to support a second professional team.

This was the situation in 1900 when Bancroft Johnson decided to challenge the high-flying National League by turning his fledgling Western League into a major league. His original plans did not call for a team in Boston, but with the financial backing of Charles Somers, a wealthy coal, lumber and shipping magnate, a team was set up early in the winter of 1901. Land was purchased out on Huntington Avenue and ground was broken in March for a new ballpark. With its new team, Boston was ready to take on anyone in the rest of the American League (made up that first year of Chicago, Detroit, Cleveland, Philadel-

phia, Baltimore,Washington and Milwaukee).

The new team's name was to remain something of a puzzle during its first years. Sometimes they were known simply as "the Bostons," but this only served to confuse them with the Braves. Sometimes they

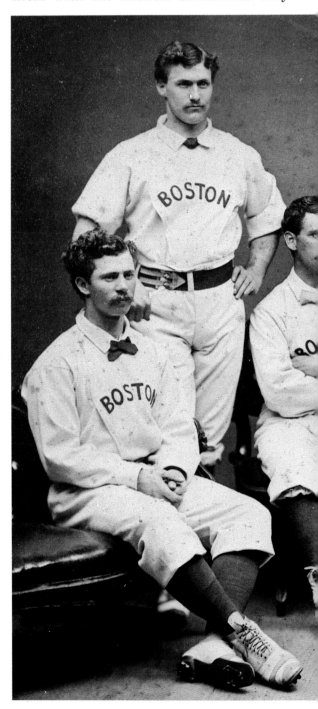

were called "the Somersets," presumably a pun on the name of the first owner, Charles Somers. At other times they were called "the Puritans" or "the Pilgrims" or even the "Plymouth Rocks." It would not be until 1907 that they adopted the name "Red Sox," the Boston Nationals having given up wearing red stockings and so allowing this link to the historic first Red Stockings to pass to an American League team. For the sake of clarity it is easier just to refer to these pre-1907 teams simply as the Red Sox.

Famed Jimmy Collins, hailed as one of the greatest third basemen in baseball history, was lured to the Red Sox from the Boston Nationals (or Beaneaters). He was paid $4000 to be player-manager, a lot more than he was earning from the Nationals. Several of the best new players were also bought out from the Boston Nationals – Chick Stahl, Buck Freeman and pitcher Ed "Parson" Lewis. The Red Sox also went after players on the St. Louis Cardinals and landed a pitcher Denton "Cy" Young. Along with Cy came his catcher, Lou Criger, and another pitcher, George Cuppy.

The Red Sox had to start their first year on the road, as the new ballpark wasn't finished, and they lost their first game 10-6 to the Baltimore Orioles. In fact, Boston lost its first four games in 1901, with Cy Young finally getting Boston's first victory, 8-6, over Connie Mack's Philadelphia Athletics on April 30. The Red Sox lost four out of five during their second week, too, before coming home to the new ballpark. The grandstand seated 2600 and the bleachers 6500, but there was lots of stand-

The 1874 Boston club won its third consecutive National Association title. Al Spalding (back row, holding ball) won 52 games and lost just 18 as the team's pitching ace.

Right: *Jimmy Collins was the player-manager for the newly-formed Boston Somersets (Red Sox) in 1901.*

Below right: *Cy Young was the winning pitcher in the Somersets' first victory. Denton True Young's nickname was a shortened version of "cyclone" – an apt description of his pitching.*

ing room. The first game, on May 8, attracted 11,000, with fans standing all around the field. That same day the Boston Nationals played at home against Brooklyn and drew only 2000. The Red Sox, with Cy Young pitching, beat the Athletics 12-4 in their home debut.

The Bosox were in the thick of the race right up until September, when the Chisox pulled away and won the first American League pennant. Boston finished second, however, 79-57, four games back, and the team had drawn 289,448 fans at home. The Red Sox topped the league in team batting at .293, led by Buck Freeman's .346. Cy Young was 31-10 that season.

In 1902 the Red Sox picked up pitcher Bill Dinneen from the Boston Nationals but finished 77-60, in third place, 6½ games behind the champion Philadelphia Athletics. In 1903 the Red Sox improved the ballpark and raised the price of tickets in the third base stands to 50 cents, while leaving it 25 cents for the rightfield seats. This done, the team proceeded to take the 1903 pennant. The Athletics had stayed close during the first half of the season, but in the end they were 16½ games behind.

The National League had finally come around to accepting that the American League was here to stay, so the first World Series was scheduled, with the Red Sox to face the Pittsburgh Pirates. The Boston players threatened to strike over compensation for the Series, but they relented when they were promised a bigger slice of the gate receipts, and the five-of-nine Series began. A standing-room-only crowd of 16,242 at Boston saw the Red Sox and Cy

Young lose the opener 7-3, but Boston – with Dinneen pitching two shutouts – went on to win five of the next seven games and became the first World Champions of modern baseball.

At the end of the 1903 season the Boston Red Sox team was sold to General Charles Henry Taylor, publisher of the *Boston Globe*. He bought the team for his son, John I. Taylor, then considered something of a playboy but a lover of sport. In 1904 the Red Sox won the pennant again, with a 95-59 record that put them just 1½ games ahead of the New York Highlanders, who had replaced Baltimore in the league and would soon be renamed the Yankees. The Rivalry had begun.

There was supposed to be a truce between the National and American Leagues by now, but John T. Brush, owner of the New York Giants, was especially bitter over the new American League team in New York, so when the Red Sox won the pennant again

in 1904, Brush declined to let his National League champions accept the challenge for a second World Series. Fan displeasure forced Brush to back down in his attitude towards the Series the following year, but unfortunately for Boston, it was not the Red Sox who were destined to confront New York in 1905.

Although 1905 had begun with great optimism in Boston, the Red Sox finished 78-74, in fourth place, 16 games behind Philadelphia. In 1906, the bottom fell out as the Red Sox' 49-105 left them 49½ games back of Chicago. Manager Jimmy Collins, not surprisingly, was replaced in August by Chick Stahl.

In 1907 the team officially became the Red Sox, but the name change was only part of a hectic season. It began in spring training when manager Stahl drank some carbolic acid – evidently committing suicide because of despondency over his personal and professional affairs. Taylor named Cy Young as manager, but at the start of the season Young said he could not be both a good pitcher *and* a manager, so

Taylor then named George Huff, athletic director at the University of Illinois and a scout for the Chicago Cubs. But Huff soon feuded with John Taylor and went back to Illinois on May 1. Next it was the turn of Boston infielder Bob Unglaub, who lasted less than a month and was replaced by veteran catcher Jim McGuire. McGuire finished out 1907, with the team ending up 59-90, in seventh place, 23 back of Detroit.

McGuire started the 1908 season as manager but gave way in August to former outfielder-catcher Fred Lake, a native Bostonian. The year 1908 turned out to be a transition time for the Red Sox. They had only a mediocre 78-79 record, finishing 15½ behind Detroit, but there were to be massive changes in personnel because John Taylor went out and spent a lot of money. Ed Cicotte, Smokey Joe Wood and an outfielder by the name of Tristram Speaker were brought in. And over the winter Taylor traded the 41-year-old Cy Young to Cleveland, despite his 21-11 record and 1.25 ERA. Some claimed Taylor got drunk with the Cleveland owner and didn't know what

Above: *The Huntington Avenue Ball Field was the site of the first World Series as the Boston Somersets went on to defeat Pittsburgh five games to three. Boston hurler Bill Dinneen was the star.*

Outfielder Tris Speaker joined the Boston outfield in 1907 but did not earn much playing time until the 1909 season. From then until he left Boston in 1916, The Grey Eagle batted over .300 each year. Speaker was elected to the Hall of Fame in 1937.

he was doing; others claim he felt Young was too old and that the Sox should be committed to youth.

In any case, Boston went into 1909 without the last remaining member of its original American League team, Cy Young. That season, Young won 19 for Cleveland, while Boston finished in third place, 88-63, 10½ behind Detroit. Fred Lake was let go as manager when he demanded a big raise, and Patsy Donovan, an old outfielder who had been managing various teams, took over. With a new and speedy team, the Red Sox were favored in 1910, but they finished in fourth, 21 back of the champion Philadelphia A's. Yet Speaker hit .340, and a crack Sox outfield – perhaps one of the greatest in baseball history – had been put together, with Speaker in center, Duffy Lewis in left and Harry Hooper in right.

Still, the next year, 1911, also proved to be a disappointment, the team going 78-75, 24

in back of the A's, who again won it all. Smokey Joe Wood won 23, including a no-hitter on July 29 against the Browns at Boston. On the last roadtrip to St. Louis, Wood had another no-hitter through 8⅔ innings, but then Burt Shotton got a single. Wood was only 21 years old.

A new era for Red Sox baseball began in 1912 with the opening of a new ballpark. The feeling had been that the Red Sox had outgrown the Huntington Avenue grounds, so the Taylors were looking for a new site. They found one at Lansdowne and Jersey Streets, in the Fenway section of Boston, a pleasant residential area not clogged with traffic. Equally persuasive, the land was owned by a realty company of which General Taylor was a large stockholder. It probably never occurred to the men responsible that the ballpark would still be there and going strong more than 75 years later. Construction began in 1911, and the park hosted its first game on April 19, 1912, when the Red Sox played Harvard in an exhibition game. And, yes, there *was* a wall cutting off left field, but it was not as high (or green) as the "Green Monster" of later years.

The first regular season game at Fenway Park was played on April 20, 1912, with the Red Sox defeating the New York Highlanders 7-6. But the big story of that day was the sinking of the *Titanic*, so the Red Sox and their new park were inside stories even in the Boston newspapers, even though 27,000 showed up for that first game. The new park was formally dedicated on May 17, a day when the Chicago White Sox beat Boston 5-2.

Though Boston now had itself a fine new park and a solid team, John Taylor sold 50 percent of the shares to Jim McAleer, an official of the Washington team, and to Bob McRoy, secretary of the American League. Jake Stahl, former catcher for the Red Sox and Washington (and brother of Chick), was named manager, and he and the Red Sox had a grand season. The team avoided injuries, and 597,096 fans checked into Fenway Park to see a team that won 109 games take the pennant, 14 games ahead of Washington. Smokey Joe Wood set a Red Sox record with his 34-5 and 1.91 ERA season. The Red Sox then faced John McGraw's New York Giants in the World Series, now down to the four-out-of-seven format. Wood struck out 11 and the Sox won the opener 4-3, and then went on to defeat the Giants in the seventh game to become the World Champions. It was a sweet revenge for the insult of 1904.

The 1913 Red Sox fell back to fourth place, 15½ games behind the Athletics, so Jake Stahl was fired and replaced by Bill

The 1912 World Series featured the Red Sox against the New York Giants. Giants' manager John McGraw and Boston skipper Jake Stahl meet with the umpires before game one.

Carrigan, the big catcher from Holy Cross, in nearby Worcester. Ban Johnson, founder-president of the American League, irate at the firing of Stahl, arranged for Joseph Lannin, a Boston and New York real estate and hotel man, to buy up McAleer's and McRoy's interest in the team.

The next year, 1914, was not a good one for the Red Sox, but it was the year of one of their greatest acquisitions. The Baltimore Orioles were a minor league team by then, and the minors were being badly hurt by the new Federal League, which was trying to become a third major league. The competition shoved salaries way up, and the Orioles had money troubles. They also had some good players, so the owner tried to peddle them to the American League. Lannin bought three players for $8000: a good catcher named Ben Egan, a good right-handed pitcher named Ernie Shore and a tall lefthanded pitcher named George Herman Ruth. They were assigned to the minor

league team in Providence and were a big hit.

Even as these newcomers were doing well at Providence, the Red Sox climbed to 91-62, 8½ games in back of the Philadelphia Athletics. Attendance was up to 481,359, best in the league. In 1915 the Sox won 101 games and beat out Detroit for the pennant by a game and a half. Tris Speaker hit .322, while the young lefthander up from Providence hit .315, led the team with his four homeruns and won 18 games. In the World Series the Red Sox took on the Phillies, and although Grover Cleveland Alexander outdueled Ernie Shore in the first game 3-1, the Sox went on to win the next four and were once more World Champions.

In 1916 the Red Sox won 91 games and lost 63, beating out Chicago by two games to take the pennant. But they had to do so without Speaker, who had become embroiled in a salary dispute. When the Federal League had been pushing salaries up Speaker had earned $18,000 in both 1914 and 1915; now, with the Federal League gone, the Red Sox cut Speaker's salary to $9000. He held out and was traded to Cleveland for Sad Sam Jones, a pitcher who would later become a star, and infielder Fred Mitchell. Boston fans were stunned, and attendance dropped. But even though Speaker hit .386 for Cleveland, leading the league, Boston had taken the pennant and went on to defeat Brooklyn in the World Series four games to one.

1917 was an unusual year for the Red Sox. First, Joe Lannin decided to sell the team; he had gradually bought up much of the Taylor family's interest but was finding ownership too demanding. So Lannin sold the team to a successful Broadway producer of musical comedies, Harry Frazee, and the repercussions of that deal would be felt in Boston for many years to come. But Frazee seemed all right in 1917, since he announced that "nothing was too good for Boston fans." And under its new manager, Jack Barry, Boston did well in 1917, for although the first World War had begun, it hadn't yet affected major league baseball very much. The Red Sox battled the Chicago White Sox for the pennant and finally lost by 10 games, even though Ruth posted 24 wins. Ruth had also participated in one of the strangest pitching records in baseball history. On June 23 he had started on the mound against Washington. The leadoff hitter, Eddie Foster, was given a fourth called ball, and Ruth was so incensed that he stormed to the plate to protest to umpire Brick Owens and ended up punching Owens. Ruth was thrown out, of course, and Eddie Shore was called in. Foster was then thrown out trying to steal, and Shore retired the next 26 in a row. Shore was thus credited with the first no-hitter pitched by a non-starter.

There was to be one more great year for these Red Sox, even though the USA was now in the world war and many players had to go into the armed services. Boston lost its manager, Barry, to the Navy, and Ed Barrow, former president of the International League, took over. Frazee, flush with money at this time, bought up some solid players, such as first baseman Stuffy McInnis, catcher Wally Schang, centerfielder Amos Strunk and pitcher Joe Bush. With Carl Mays winning 21 games, Bush 15, Sad Sam Jones 16 and Ruth 13, the Red Sox beat

out Cleveland by two games to take the pennant. Ruth hit .300, with 11 homers and 66 RBIs. Boston then went on to defeat the Chicago Cubs in the World Series 4-2. It was not until the eighth inning of the fourth game that Ruth ended his Series record of 29 ⅔ scoreless innings.

Ruth's conduct on and off field was erratic and Frazee began to sell off players such as Ernie Shore and Dutch Leonard. Frazee then got into a salary fight with Ruth, who eventually signed for $10,000 and went on to set a record with his 29 homers. The temperamental pitcher Carl Mays walked off the mound in a game after the Sox made two errors and put him behind, and, over Ban Johnson's protests, Frazee sold Mays to the Yankees. The Red Sox ended up with a 66-71 record, 20½ games behind the Chicago White Sox, who would go on to have their own troubles in the infamous "Black Sox" Series. But for the Red Sox, the shape of things to come had been prefigured by Frazee's ominous willingness to sell good players.

Top: *The Cubs' Fred Merkle is forced out at third base in game four of the 1918 World Series.*

Above: *Avid Boston fans known as the Royal Rooters cheered for Boston teams in both leagues. The Royal Rooters, who rooted the Red Sox to a Series championship in 1912, are shown here at the Boston Braves' 1914 World Series.*

Left: *Dutch Leonard warms up before his start in the 1916 Series' fourth game. In his complete-game, 6-2 victory, Leonard allowed no runs and only three hits after the first inning.*

2. A Team Dismantled

It was called "the rape of the Red Sox," and it could not have been more devastating to Red Sox fans if the entire city of Boston had been brought under siege. In one fell swoop Harry Frazee assumed, in the eyes of fans, the image of a modern-day Benedict Arnold.

Perhaps it should have been obvious to those close to the team, or at least those close to Frazee. For Frazee was not a long-term baseball man who had deep associations with Boston or the Red Sox. He was a native of Peoria, Illinois, who had been bitten early by the bug to get to the big city and make big deals. He had begun as a bellhop and, through some shrewd dealings, had become a successful theatrical producer and theater owner in New York and Chicago. That, not baseball, was his true life.

When he bought the Red Sox from Joseph Lannin in early 1917 Frazee had little ready cash. He bought on credit, writing notes for most of the $1 million purchase price, and he expected to pay off the notes with profits from the team. Lannin reportedly had made $400,000 profit in three years, and when the Red Sox captured the World Series in 1918 it looked as though Frazee's gamble was going to pay off.

But if Frazee's baseball investment was paying dividends, his theatrical investments were not. He kept picking lemons to back, and his cash flow began to dry up. Creditors who held the paper notes Frazee had signed so blithely were making noises, including the people who owned Fenway Park. Even when fans came out in droves during the 1919 season to watch Babe Ruth set a new record with his 29 home runs for the season Frazee was nearing the bottom of his financial barrel. And one way or another, it was affecting his team. When someone asked Ruth what Frazee had given him for hitting his homers, Ruth snorted, "A cigar."

It so happened that Frazee's office in New York was two doors down from Jacob Ruppert's Yankees office. The two team owners occasionally went out to lunch together. Ruppert realized that Frazee was having

Right: *The hated Red Sox owner from 1917 to 1923, Harry Frazee. To finance his theatrical productions, Frazee sold 11 Red Sox players, including Babe Ruth, to the rival Yankees.*

money troubles, and if there was one thing Jake Ruppert had, it was money from his profitable brewery. And if there was one thing Jake Ruppert wanted more than money, it was to make the Yankees powerful and successful.

And so, on January 9, 1920, Ruppert called a press conference in New York. To the gathered media, he said: "Gentlemen, we have just bought Babe Ruth from Harry Frazee of the Boston Red Sox." At the same time, Frazee's Red Sox office was giving the same message to the Boston media. In the tumult that ensued Frazee at first tried to make some lame excuses. Ruth's record-breaking 29 home runs, he said, "were more spectacular than useful. They didn't help get the Red Sox out of sixth place." But in the end he had to admit that he just plain needed the money.

And it *was* a substantial sum. Reports put it at $125,000, a huge amount in those days for a player. (Ruppert had bought Carl Mays from the Red Sox for $40,000.) But the actual price was bigger than that. In addition to the $125,000 in cash, Frazee extracted a $350,000 mortgage on Fenway Park, enabling him to keep his creditors at bay and still pump money into his theatrical productions.

Ruth was as shocked as anyone. "I always have liked Boston and its fans," he said. But he, too, did well financially. The Yankees tore up his $10,000 contract and gave him a new one for $20,000. He paid it back with interest when he hit 54 homers in his first year in New York, and the Yankees drew 1,289,422 fans, a record for all baseball at the time. True, the Yankees finished third in 1920, three in back of the pennant-winning Indians, but they were 23 games ahead of the fifth-place Boston.

Ruppert was happy with Ruth's first season but still felt his team needed more new blood. Now that he had opened the line to Frazee, he proceeded to tap it. Frazee sent the Yankees catcher Wally Schang, a promising New York schoolboy pitcher named Waite Hoyt, Harry Harper, a lefthanded pitcher, and utility outfielder Mike McNally. In return, the Red Sox got some mediocre players and a kid named Muddy Ruel, who the Yankees didn't think was big enough to stand the strain of catching 150 big league games a year. There was also some more cash for Frazee to keep the creditors away a bit longer.

Ruel would surprise everyone by becoming a top catcher for eight seasons with the Red Sox, but the best the new manager,

Yankee owner Jacob Ruppert (center left) plays host to New York Governor Alfred Smith and wife at Yankee Stadium opening day in 1923. This was the year that Ruppert's association with Sox owner Frazee would pay off: the Yankees won the Series and the Red Sox finished last.

Waite Hoyt was traded to the Yankees in 1921 after two seasons with the Red Sox. Although Hoyt's performance for the Red Sox was unspectacular, the future Hall of Famer would go on to have a long and successful career.

Hugh Duffy, could do in 1921 was to bring the Sox in in fifth place again. The Yankees, meanwhile, finally won their pennant, with 98 wins. Ruth hit 59 homers and had 171 RBIs and a .378 average. Yet the Yankees lost to the New York Giants in the World Series, and Ruppert again went back to the obliging Frazee for more players. This time Frazee sold two top pitchers, Sad Sam Jones and Bullet Joe Bush; they would join two other former Red Sox pitchers, Carl Mays, who had won 27 for the Yankees in 1921, and Waite Hoyt, who had won 19.

In 1922 the Yankees were in a tough race with the St. Louis Browns for the flag, so the Yankees went to Frazee yet again and this time bought Jumping Joe Dugan, an outstanding shortstop, and outfielder Elmer Smith. It cost Ruppert $50,000, but it gained the Yankees another pennant.

The St. Louis Chamber of Commerce was so outraged at this that it initiated a letter-writing campaign to the new Commissioner of Baseball, Kenesaw Mountain Landis. Largely as a result, the major leagues adopted a rule that no deals for players could be made after June 15 of each season (except for players placed on waivers for the low waiver price).

Despite their star-studded lineup, the Yankees again lost to the Giants in the World Series. Ruppert decided that what the team needed now was a lefthanded pitcher, and who had a better one than Harry Frazee, with his Herb Pennock, winner of 10 games for the Red Sox in 1922. So Pennock went to New York, and Frazee got another check. When Frazee also sold a top prospect from the farm system, right-handed pitcher George Pipgras, there was little more left in Boston.

The Yanks took the pennant again in 1923, with 98 wins, Pennock accounting for 19 of them, and they finally beat the Giants in the World Series. Boston, with its new manager, Frank Chance of Chicago Cubs fame, came in dead last, 61-91. Red Sox attendance plummeted to 229,000.

At long last the despoiler was driven away. With nothing left to sell, Frazee could no longer look to Ruppert to write him checks. And since the Boston fans now hated him so much that they were staying away in droves, he could only lose more money. Finally, in July, 1923, Ban Johnson, founder-president of the American League, arranged for J. A. Robert "Bob" Quinn, vice president and business manager of the St. Louis Browns, to buy the Red Sox. Quinn himself didn't have much money, but he scraped together enough to buy what Frazee had left of a once great team. The purchase had left Quinn with little cash, and when his major financial "angel" died he was left in precarious straits.

Ironically, the very next year Frazee finally hit it big on Broadway. His show *No, No, Nanette* was a huge success, and he made millions – too late for Boston. The Yankee dynasties of the 1920s and 1930s, and perhaps beyond, might well have belonged to the Red Sox if *No, No, Nanette* had come along earlier. In any event, Harry Frazee himself didn't have long to enjoy his success. A couple of years later, at the age of only 48, he died.

The Yankees and the Red Sox continued to go in opposite directions. In 1924 Boston was 67-85, 28 games out of first. In 1925 it was 47-105, 49½ games out. And in 1926 it was 46-107, 44½ out. Lee Fohl managed the team for those three dismal years, and if all these problems weren't enough for him, part of Fenway Park burned down in May 8, 1926. The bleachers along the left field foul line were totally destroyed, and because the club had no money, they weren't replaced, making it possible for fielders to chase foul flies behind the third base grandstand.

Lee Fohl was replaced in 1927 by Bill Carrigan, who had quit in 1916 but came back now because Quinn was trying to give the Red Sox some credibility. Bill had won the pennant in 1916, but in 1927 he could only finish 51-103, 59 games behind the Yankees. In 1928, it was 57-96, 43½ back, and in 1919, 58-96, 48 behind. Carrigan gave way to Charles Wagner in 1930, but the team was still 52-103, 50 behind the pennant-winning Philadelphia A's.

Harry Frazee was long gone, but his legacy cost the Red Sox still another pitcher who helped continue the Yankee Dynasty. Almost out of cash, Bob Quinn sold Red Ruffing to the Yankees in 1930 for a reported $50,000. Ruffing became a key contributor to most of the Yankees' pennant drives in the 1930s.

In 1931 Wagner was replaced by Shano Collins, star of earlier great teams in Chicago. He had joined the Red Sox in 1921 and had finished out his playing career in 1925. But it wasn't much better for Collins in 1931 than it had been for Wagner, the Red Sox going 62-90, still 45 games behind the Athletics. In the middle of the 1932 season, Collins gave way to Martin McManus, and the team ended at an all-time low, 43-111, a win percentage of only .279, 64 in back of the pennant-winning Yankees. Only 182,150 fans showed up for that season. But amid all this darkness, a white knight was riding out of New York to rescue the Red Sox. His name was Tom Yawkey.

Bullet Joe Bush won 26 games for the Yankees in 1922 after being sold by Red Sox owner Harry Frazee – only one of six Boston pitchers sold by the unpopular owner. Bush won 62 games in three years with Jacob Ruppert's Yankees.

3. Yawkey Rebuilds a Team

The Red Sox had hit rock bottom in 1932. Bob Quinn, the owner, also bottomed out in 1932. Not wealthy when he took over the team, he had seen what little money he had, and what little he could borrow, go down the drain. There was little talent on the team, scant hope of improvement and no more money. The bank holiday that was a low point of the Depression left Quinn with no other sources of revenue than his insurance policies. Quinn borrowed on them to have enough money to pay the bills for spring training in 1933, but he had no idea where the money would come from to see the team through the rest of the season. Then along came Tom Yawkey, riding a horse of greenbacks, and Red Sox baseball was saved.

Tom Yawkey had wanted to own a baseball team for years. Perhaps it was the result of hearing his uncle, Bill Yawkey, talk about the times he had when he owned the early Detroit Tigers. In any case, Yawkey loved baseball, and when he was at Yale he played second base for the Elis. When he came of age Tom inherited a $500,000 trust fund. Later he inherited $4 million from his late mother's estate and then $3.4 million from his foster father's estate. More than that, he inherited the family business of lumber and metals in Canada. By the time he was 30 Tom Yawkey was a full-fledged multimillionaire.

He bought the Red Sox for about $1 million, enabling Quinn to liquidate all the debts he had incurred running the team but leaving him with no money of his own. "I was broke and out of a job," Quinn said, "but I was free of debt. I breathed a sigh of relief when it was over."

Yawkey was off and running as soon as he touched down at Fenway Park. "I don't intend to mess around with a loser," Yawkey said, and Red Sox fans took heart, especially when Yawkey hired respected former Athletics and White Sox star Eddie Collins as his vice president and general manager. Yawkey also let it be known that he would spend millions to make his new acquisition successful. In token of this, he promised to rebuild Fenway Park, which had undergone little structural change since it was built in 1912. He vowed it would be one of the best-looking ball parks in the major leagues.

Although Yawkey didn't take over the Sox until April 20, 1933, and thus could make no deal to strengthen the team for that season, his mere arrival on the scene seemed to help. The Sox went from 43-111 in 1932 to 63-86 in 1933. Then the changes really began. The first was the ballpark itself. Fire had burned down some of the wooden bleachers in left field, and when work was begun to replace them, another fire burned the centerfield bleachers. Yawkey therefore decided to make it a fireproof park of cement and steel. Yawkey also wanted to enlarge the leftfield bleachers so that they would be a continuation of the centerfield ones. Since there was not enough land, he discussed with Boston city officials the possibility of acquiring some of Lansdowne Street to allow the bleachers to curve around to the left. Despite his offer to buy the street, the city declined, and the famous leftfield wall, the Green Monster, was the result, the only way the engineers could maintain the lines on the ballpark. It probably cost 3500 seats and set up different dimensions for the park, but at least it did provide baseball with one of its most famous and best recognized monuments.

The ballpark that had held as many as

The Red Sox were saved in 1933 when Tom Yawkey purchased the club. Here, Mr. and Mrs. Yawkey take in the opening game of the 1934 season.

41,000 in pre-renovation days now had a seating capacity of 34,000 and standing room for many others, until fire laws cut deeply into the standing-room.

The ballpark renovation reportedly cost $750,000, but it was just the beginning of what Yawkey meant to spend to rebuild the team. And since Eddie Collins had been an executive with Connie Mack at the Philadelphia Athletics, who better to approach for some deals than Connie?

Connie Mack had a superb team in Philadelphia in the early 1930s, but for some reason the Philadelphia fans did not respond wholeheartedly, and Mack had financial troubles. Thus he was happy enough to get $125,000 of Yawkey's money and two second-line players in exchange for lefthanded pitchers Lefty Grove and Rube Walberg and second baseman Max Bishop.

Grove was 33 years old, but he was 24-8 in 1933. He only managed 8-8 for Boston in 1934, and Connie Mack was embarrassed enough to offer to refund Yawkey's money. But Tom stuck with the deal, and Grove became a winner for Boston, winning 20 in 1935, 17 each in 1936 and 1937, 14 in 1938 and 15 in 1939.

Bishop played two years with Boston and then retired; Walberg had four sub-.500 years with Boston and also retired. But Yawkey, meantime, was still dealing. He had acquired Stanley "Bucky" Harris as a manager, replacing Marty McManus, inherited from Bob Quinn. Then he got fiery Wes Ferrell, a controversial character but a fine pitcher. He had been a star for Cleveland, but he had had a disagreement with the Indians, so Cleveland sent him to Boston for two players and $25,000. He won 14 for Boston in 1934, 25 in 1935 and 20 in 1936, and into the bargain he was reunited with his brother, catcher Rick Ferrell, who had come to Boston in May of 1933 from the St. Louis Browns for a player and cash.

Yawkey also purchased shortstop Lynn Lary from the Yankees and lefthanded pitcher Fritz Ostermueller from the Cardinals' farm team at a hefty price. The Sox improved to .500 in 1934, with 76-76 mark and 610,000 fans. Yawkey was clearly making progress.

And the progress continued. After the 1934 season he bought a new shortstop-manager. Joe Cronin was Washington's playing manager and was considered one of the top shortstops in the league, so Yawkey paid Clark Griffith $250,000 for Cronin and threw in Lynn Lary for the deal. Since Cronin was Griffith's son-in-law, the trade stirred considerable interest.

Cronin was to manage the Sox for 12 seasons and be one of the top shortstops in the league for six of those seasons. Cronin's first season with Yawkey's "Millionaires," as they were now being called, was two games better than the 1934 finish, but 78-75 still left the Sox in fourth place behind the great Yankees.

Cronin did inadvertently supply one of the plays that would have made the day's highlight films if they had had them in 1935. It came in a game against Cleveland. Boston had scored twice in the ninth to cut a Cleveland lead to 5-3. The Sox had the bases loaded and no out when Cronin lashed a drive down the third base line. It hit third baseman Odell Hale on the head and caromed in the air to the shortstop, who caught it for the out and then tossed it to the

Above left: *Tom Yawkey hired Eddie Collins (right, alongside George Sisler) to take over vice president and general manager duties.*

Below: *Fenway Park after Yawkey's renovations. The rebuilt park seated fewer fans, but sported the notorious "Green Monster" – the left field wall.*

second baseman for an out at second. A relay to first then tripled off the other runner.

In 1936 the Sox made several shopping trips to Philadelphia, coming up with slugging first baseman Jimmie Foxx and pitcher John Marcum for $150,000, as well as with Roger "Doc" Cramer, centerfielder,

and infielder Eric McNair for $75,000. But the "Gold Sox" nevertheless finished at 74-80, sixth in the league, 28½ behind New York.

It was getting a little frustrating, but Yawkey kept trying. He traded disruptive, if effective, Wes Ferrell and brother Rick to Washington for Ben Chapman, a speedy outfielder, and for righthander Bobo Newsom. Yawkey also was thinking about building a farm system, seeing how well the Yankees and Cardinals were doing by growing their own players. He sent new farm director Billy Evans to the West Coast, where a lot of minor league teams had developed players and had sold them to the big league teams. The Yankees had picked up Joe DiMaggio in San Francisco, and the Red Sox found second baseman Bobby Doerr in Los Angeles and outfielder Ted Williams in San Diego. Another kid in San Francisco got the nod from Boston, Dom DiMaggio, who had replaced brother Joe in center for the San Francisco Seals. Meanwhile, Jos Vosmik, a slugging outfielder, was obtained from St. Louis for Bobo Newsom and two others. Newsom had feuded with Cronin the previous year.

The 1938 Red Sox finished higher than any Sox team since 1918, in second place at 88-61, 11 behind the Yankees. Foxx led the league with his .349 average, with 50 homers and 175 RBIs. The 1939 Red Sox

Opposite: *The Red Sox picked up first sacker Jimmie Foxx from Philadelphia in 1936. During his six seasons with Boston, the future Hall of Famer hit fewer than 30 home runs only once.*

Left: *Second baseman Bobby Doerr began a Hall of Fame career in Boston in 1937.*

Below: *Manager Joe Cronin (pointing) looks over the Yankee Stadium diamond prior to the 1939 opener. With the Red Sox skipper are (left to right) rookies Emerson Dickman, Ted Williams, James Tabor and Woodrow Rich.*

Right: *Dom DiMaggio makes a leaping catch in front of the outfield wall. DiMaggio batted .301 as a rookie for the Red Sox in 1940.*

Opposite above: *Sox shortstop Johnny Pesky poses with Lt. Commander Edward S. Brewer (right). After a promising rookie year (1942) in which he led the league with 205 hits, Pesky joined the U.S. Navy.*

Opposite below: *Ted Williams belts a triple at Fenway against the Senators on August 11, 1941, on his way to procuring a .406 season batting average. The Thumper lost three years to World War II.*

were 89-62, 17 behind the Yankees, who won 106 games and had seven pitchers in double figures in wins, led by former Red Soxer Red Ruffing, with 21. Lefty Grove won 15 for the Sox, who had three others with 11 wins each. And their hitting was even better, led by Foxx at .360, with 35 homers and 105 RBIs.

Everyone, however, was talking about a 6-foot, 3-inch, skinny (180 pounds) kid in right field, up from Minneapolis, where he had hit .366 the previous year. Rookie Ted Williams batted .327, hit 31 homers and led the league in RBIs, with 145. As New York Yankee Hall of Fame catcher Bill Dickey summed it up after the first game he saw Williams play: "He's just a damned good hitter."

The next year, 1940, the Sox broke their attendance record as 716,234 paid their way into Fenway. It was a remarkable year for many things, including the fact that the Yankees were dethroned by the Detroit Tigers, whose top pitcher, believe it or not, was Bobo Newsom, with a 21-5 mark. The Tigers won 90, edging Cleveland, whose Bob Feller won 27. The Yankees finished at 88-66, two back, as Ruffing dipped to just 15 wins. Dom DiMaggio moved into right field for Boston and hit .301 in his rookie season, while Williams hit .344, with 23 homers and 113 RBIs. Cronin was putting on weight

and slowing down, but he still hit .285, with 24 homers and 111 RBIs. Foxx was at .297, with 36 homers and 119 RBIs.

In 1941 the Red Sox finished second, with 84 wins, but 17 behind the Yankees, who had 101 wins and were led by Joe DiMaggio, who had a .357 average, with 30 homers and 125 RBIs, as well as a record that still stands in baseball: hitting safely in 56 consecutive games. Williams ended the season entering the exclusive club of .400 hitters, finishing at .406, with 37 homers and 120 RBIs and sharing the spotlight with Joe D's remarkable 56-game hitting streak.

Williams had gone into that last day hitting an even .400, and Cronin offered to sit him out to preserve it. Instead, he insisted on playing a doubleheader with Philadelphia, and the 23-year-old had six hits in eight trips, to end at .406 but second to the Yankee Clipper in the voting for most valuable player.

War clouds darkened the scene for the 1942 season. The Red Sox won 93 games and had a .612 winning percentage, yet they still finished nine in back of the Yanks, who won 103 games. Tony Lupien, an Ivy Leaguer from Harvard, became the Sox' first baseman, Jimmie Foxx having been waived to the Chicago Cubs. Williams hit .356, 36 homers and 137 RBIs, leading the league in all three categories. But baseball writers showed they could be vindictive when they voted Joe Gordon of the Yankees the MVP, Ted losing by one vote because one New York writer wouldn't put Williams even among the top five in the league. Ted Williams and the writers had feuded ever since his rookie season of 1939.

Now the war took its toll. Williams, Pesky and DiMaggio left after the 1942 season. Tex Hughson, who had won 22 games in 1942, and Doerr went in 1944. The patchwork team that was left finished seventh in 1943, fourth in 1944 and seventh in 1945, when the only bright spot was a right-handed pitcher from Mississippi who was discharged from the Army because of asthma. David "Boo" Ferriss was 21-10 for the 1945 Sox, but one and all were waiting for the war to end and the 1946 season to begin.

4. Glory and Decline

Finally it happened. After 13 years of waiting by Tom Yawkey and 28 by Red Sox fans, Boston won the pennant in 1946.

Doerr, Pesky, Williams, Hughson, DiMaggio and pitcher Joe Dobson had come home from the wars, and they were ready to declare war on the rest of the American League. The Sox now made a trade with Detroit to help fill the hole at first base, getting veteran Rudy York for shortstop Eddie Lake, since Pesky had made Lake expendable. The Sox also moved veteran Mike Higgins to third base and put Catfish Metkovich in right.

They broke from the starting blocks as if they were running the 100-yard dash, put together a 15-game winning streak, won 21 of the first 25 and cruised to 104 wins and a 22-game margin over the Detroit Tigers. They clinched with a 1-0 Tex Hughson victory over Cleveland in which Williams hit an inside-the-park home run.

Hughson won 20, Ferriss 25, Mickey Harris, a lefthander, 17 and Dobson 13. York hit .276, with 17 homers and 119 RBIs. Doerr batted .271, with 18 homers and 116 RBIs. Pesky hit .335, Dom DiMaggio hit .316, and Williams had another big year: .342, 38 homers and 123 RBIs. He was finally named AL MVP. He had thrilled fans by hitting two home runs in the All-Star game

at Fenway Park off Rip Sewell's slow, arching "eephus" pitch, the second one by running up on the ball and clobbering it to center field.

This was also the year of the famed Lou Boudreau "Williams Shift," in which the Cleveland manager lined up the infield so that the third baseman was the only fielder on the left side of the infield. Ted stubbornly continued to pull the ball, despite the shift, although he did go to left for the inside-the-park homer that clinched the pennant, circling the bases before the over-shifted left-fielder could retrieve the ball.

The first World Series at Fenway Park in 28 years had the Cardinals as the opposition, St. Louis having won a playoff with the Brooklyn Dodgers two games to none. The Cards featured Stan Musial, who had a league-leading .365 average, with 16 homers and 103 RBIs, and Enos Slaughter, who had a .300 average, with 18 homers and 130 RBIs. Howie Pollet was their leading pitcher at 21-10.

Boston won the opener in 10 innings, 3-2, on York's home run. Hughson started for Boston, but Earl Johnson was the winner in relief, with Pollet the loser. Game 2 went to Harry "The Cat" Brecheen, 3-0. The Cat held the Sox to four hits. Mickey Harris gave up six hits but lost.

The Red Sox won a team-record thirteenth consecutive game when they beat Chicago 14-9 on May 8, 1946. Left to right are Dom DiMaggio, Rudy York, Johnny Pesky and Ted Williams.

Cardinal great Stan Musial is caught in a run-down between Red Sox third baseman Pinky Higgins (36) and pitcher Boo Ferriss during game three of the 1946 World Series. Ferriss shut out the Cards, 4-0, in a complete-game victory.

Boo Ferriss won Game 3, 4-0, on a six-hitter, with York hitting a three-run homer off Murry Dickson. Game 4 went to St. Louis, as the Cards battered Hughson and four others for 20 hits and a 12-3 easy win for Red Munger. Slaughter, Whitey Kurowski and Joe Garagiola, a rookie catcher, had four hits each.

Game 5 went to the Red Sox 6-3. Dobson pitched four-hit baseball and the Sox ripped 11 hits off Pollet and two others.

Game 6 went to Brecheen, as the little southpaw allowed just seven hits in a 4-1 win at St. Louis. Harris started, and Hughson came on in relief for Boston, but the Cards got eight hits. The season was down to one last game.

Game 7 will go down in World Series history as one of the most exciting and unusual. The Sox came up with two runs in the top of the eighth to tie at 3-3 in a duel with Dickson. Ferriss started, and Harris came on in the fifth, but Bob Klinger was the loser in relief when destiny nodded to St. Louis. In the last of the eighth, with Enos Slaughter on first, Harry Walker crashed a drive into the gap. Slaughter was off and running.

In the Red Sox rally in the top of the eighth Dom DiMaggio had doubled and pulled a muscle in his leg running out the hit. He couldn't play center in the last of the eighth. Leon Culberson was a good out-fielder, but not a great one like DiMaggio.

"I wouldn't have tried if Dom had been out there," Slaughter said later. But Dom was not out there, and Slaughter kept running, and when the relay came in to Pesky in short left center, he held the ball just long enough for Slaughter, going all out, to roar around third and slide under the belated throw home. The score was 4-3, Cardinals, and there it remained.

Pesky took a lot of criticism for that play, but Slaughter said it was the fault of Bobby Doerr or Higgins for not telling Pesky to throw home, since his back was to the in-field and he didn't see Slaughter rounding third.

It was an exciting Series, if a disappointing one for Sox fans. Williams hit just .220 in his only World Series appearance, and Musial hit .222. Many still wonder if Williams was affected by being hit on the elbow in an exhibition game of AL stars against Boston while the NL playoffs were underway. Hit by Mickey Haefner of Washington, Williams had had to undergo therapy for two days before the Series.

At any rate, 1947 looked like another big year for Boston, but Ferriss, Harris and Hughson all had arm trouble, and from 62 wins in 1946 they dropped to 29 in 1947. Boston finished third, with 83 wins, 21 less than in 1946 and 14 behind the Yankees. Joe Dobson was the top winner, at 18, and Williams hit .343, with 22 homers and 114 RBIs.

The 1947 season marked the end of Joe Cronin's managerial career. He was re-

Stan Musial (left) and Ted Williams pose for a photo before the All-Star game in 1948 at Sportsman's Park in St. Louis. The American League won, 5-2. Musial and Williams would lead their leagues in batting average this year.

placed by former Yankee skipper Joe McCarthy. And in December of 1947 the Sox made a big deal with the St. Louis Browns, buying Vern Stephens, Billy Hitchcock and pitchers Jack Kramer and Ellis Kinder. Kramer would lead the league in winning percentage that year. It cost $375,000, as well as a whole slew of Boston players – Eddie Pellagrini, Sam Dente, Bill Sommers, Pete Layden, Roy Partee, Don Palmer and pitchers Jim Wilson, Clem Dreisewerd, Al Widmar and Joe Ostrowski. Sam Mele had come up in 1947 as a slugging rookie, and in 1948 Billy Dale Goodman, a switch-hitting utility infielder, came up from the farm.

The Sox, Yankees and Cleveland slugged it out for the 1948 pennant, and at the end the Sox and Indians had tied at 96-58, two games ahead of the Yankees. Williams hit .369, with 25 homers and 127 RBIs. Goodman hit .310 while playing first, and Doerr was .285, with 27 homers and 111 RBIs. Stephens hit .269, with 29 homers and 137 RBIs. Joe Dobson won 16, Mel Parnell 15, Kramer 18 and Kinder 10. But when it came to the one playoff game, at Fenway Park, McCarthy picked the right-handed journeyman Denny Galehouse, who had an 8-7 record.

Cleveland bombed him 8-3. Lou Boudreau, Cleveland shortstop and manager, hit two homers and two singles. Later McCarthy said he had no rested arms and there was no one else to pitch. Parnell and Kinder have claimed they each offered to pitch and were ready to go. That 1948 playoff game remains one of the "black holes" of Boston Red Sox history.

Disappointment was destined to plague them another year, as Boston went into the 1949 season. Joe DiMaggio came back from heel surgery to demolish the Red Sox in a three-game series at Fenway Park. He hit four home runs, three of them game winners. It sent the Sox reeling, and they fell 12½ back by July 4, but they rallied and went into Yankee Stadium for the final two games of the season with a one-game lead. They needed just one win in two games and were to pitch Parnell and then Kinder. The Yanks beat Parnell 5-4, as Joe Black had a great relief appearance for New York. And so it came down to the second game. It was Kinder vs. Vic Raschi.

The Yanks led 1-0, after seven, having scored in the first. In the eighth McCarthy lifted Kinder for a pinch hitter who did not come through. Then he brought in Parnell in relief, and Parnell yielded a homer to Tommy Henrich and a single to Yogi Berra. Parnell was replaced by Hughson, who had been on the disabled list and said his arm still hurt. But he came on and, with the bases loaded, Jerry Coleman hit a soft liner that Al Zarilla in right tried to shoestring but missed, and it went for a triple and three runs.

In the ninth the Sox rallied for three runs but still fell short, and for the second year in a row McCarthy's managing was called into question. Why, said critics, with a power-laden lineup, pinch hit for Kinder? See what happened in the ninth? McCarthy was on thin ice. Hughson also claimed McCarthy ruined his career by making him pitch with a sore arm.

In 1950 the Sox were 31-31 when McCarthy resigned and retired from baseball. Steve O'Neill, a former Cleveland catcher who had managed at Cleveland and Detroit, was hired as his replacement. The team finished at 94-60, four behind the Yankees and one behind second-place Detroit. Parnell won 18, Kinder 14 and Dobson 15. A rookie first baseman from Moosup, Connecticut, arrived, and Walt Dropo was a sensation, hitting .322, with 34 homers and 144 RBIs.

Stephens also had 144 RBIs, with 30 homers and a .295 average. Doerr hit .294, with 27 homers and 120 RBIs. Williams shattered his elbow making a spectacular catch in the All-Star game and played in only 89 games, with 28 homers and 97 RBIs.

The Sox had topped the million mark in attendance for the first time in 1946, and the turnstiles continued to revolve, reaching 1,596,650 in 1949.

Williams bounced back in 1951 with a .318 average, 30 homers and 144 RBIs. But the team slumped to 87-67, 11 out of first, and attendance fell to 1,312,282. Dropo dipped to .239, with 11 homers and 57 RBIs. Doerr hit .289 in his last year, with 13 homers and 73 RBIs. Parnell won 18 and Kinder, now a reliever was 11-2, with 14 saves. Williams was then recalled by the Marines for the Korean War.

Lou Boudreau replaced O'Neill as manager, but the Sox slide continued, 76-78 in 1952, 19 back; 84-69 in 1953, 16 back; and in 1954 it was a horrendous 69-85, 42 behind the Indians, who won 110 games. Boudreau was gone, and Mike Higgins was the manager. Attendance had now fallen under the million mark for the first time since 1946.

In 1955 Williams was back from the Marines and hit .356, with 28 homers and 83 RBIs. Jackie Jensen, an outfielder picked up in a trade with Washington, led Boston with 116 RBIs and 26 homers. Frank Sullivan led Boston with 18 wins. But the team finished at 84-70, fourth place, 12 in back of the Yankees. But at least attendance topped 1.2 million.

Boston was 84-70 again in 1956, 13 behind New York. Williams led in percentages, with a .345 average. Former California football star Jackie Jensen led in runs batted in, with 97. Rookie pitcher Tom Brewer won 19. In 1957 Boston was 82-72, 16 behind New York. Williams hit .388, with 28 homers, and rookie Frank Malzone at third knocked in 103 runs, as did Jensen. But Jensen was finding baseball increasingly difficult since he hated to fly, and some distances were just too great to cover by train.

The record was 79-75 in 1958, Higgins' last full season as manager, and the team was third, 13 behind the Yanks. Williams hit .328, with 28 homers. Dick Gernert, a new first baseman, hit 20 homers and knocked in 69 runs, while Malzone had 87 RBIs. Jensen had 35 homers and 122 RBIs. Ike Delock led the pitching staff at 14-8.

In 1959 the Sox started slowly. Higgins was relieved as manager, and Billy Jurges finished up, as Boston went 75-79, 19 back of the Chicago White Sox. It was a remarkable year for a number of reasons. Williams hit under .300 for the first time in his career, coming in at .254, and Elijah

New Boston manager Joe McCarthy talks to his troops in spring training prior to the 1948 season. The Sox would lose to Cleveland in a one-game playoff to fall short.

Tex Hughson collected two 20-win seasons in eight seasons with the Red Sox. Hughson, who broke in with Boston in 1941, blamed manager McCarthy for ruining his career by making him pitch with a sore arm.

"Pumpsie" Green, an infielder, became the first black to play for the Red Sox. In 1959 the Sox also had a new centerfielder, Gary Geiger, who was traded to Boston by Cleveland for Jimmy Piersall. Piersall, a young man from Waterbury, Connecticut, had been another in a long line of outstanding centerfielders for the Red Sox. But he also had serious psychological problems that eventually hospitalized him; this experience led to the book he wrote with Al Hirshberg, *Fear Strikes Out*, in which he discussed his mental problems. It became a hit movie.

Jurges began 1960 as manager and was replaced in mid-season by Higgins again. Boston, which had gone 75-79 in 1959, went 65-89, 32 out in 1960, behind the Yankees. It was 76-86 in 1961, 33 in back of New York again, and it was 76-84 in 1962, eighth place, 19 in back of the Yankees. This was Higgins' last year as manager. He became general manager, and Pesky managed in 1963, 76-85, 28 behind New York. Billy Herman took over in the middle of 1964, when the Sox fell to 72-90, 27 back. Attendance was under 900,000 in three of the four years from 1961 to 1964 and was to drop to under 700,000 in 1965.

There were a few highlights. Williams closed his career in 1960 by hitting .316 at the age of 41; in his final at bat he homered, the 521st of his major league career. Carl Yastrzemski came up in 1961, the heir apparent to Williams, and he hit .266 in his first year, with 11 homers and 80 RBIs.

The Sox also got their second black player, pitcher Earl Wilson, who teamed with Medford native Bill Monbouquette to give Boston a good one-two pitching punch. Each pitched a no-hitter for the Sox in 1962, and Monbouquette won 20 in 1963.

The Sox of these years also featured a young fireballing reliever. Dick Radatz was a 6-foot, 6-inch 230-pounder who threw as hard as anyone in baseball. He was a huge menacing sight on the mound, tugging at the tiny cap that was too small for his head. He was called The Monster, and fans loved to come see him. There weren't too many other reasons to come see the Sox in those years. Radatz lasted four remarkable years with Boston and then was traded.

During these eight dark years in the second division Pete Runnels was one of the few bright lights, hitting over .300 in five of his seven years with Boston and leading the league twice, in 1960 at .320 and in 1962 at .326. Dick Stuart, whose fielding earned him the name of Stone Fingers, hit 42 homers and drove in 118 in 1963, but he also led the league in errors, with 29 at first. In 1964 Tony Conigliaro came up, and the young man from nearby Swampscott hit 24 homers as a 19-year-old. In 1965 Yaz hit .312, and a pitcher by the name of Jim Lonborg won nine games.

Yet despite some notable individual achievements, these had been arid years for Red Sox fans, and by 1965 attendance at Fenway Park had dropped well below 700,000. Nor were prospects for the future particularly bright. That there could be a rapid reversal of the club's fortunes seemed impossible . . . no more than a dream.

Left: *Red Sox skipper Bill Jurges welcomes infielder Pumpsie Green in July of 1959. Green was the first black to ever play for Boston.*

Below: *Jimmy Piersall is tagged out at the plate by Kansas City catcher Hal Smith in a 1957 contest. Piersall played the Sox outfield from 1950 to 1958.*

5. The Impossible Dream

The year 1965 would appear an unlikely candidate for the turnaround year for the Red Sox after 15 years of going nowhere in the American League. The highlight of 1965 had been the no-hit game pitched by Dave Morehead against the Cleveland Indians on September 16. (That was the last no-hitter by a Red Sox hurler.) That and a 20-year-old outfielder by the name of Tony Conigliaro gave Boston's disappointed fans what little they had to cheer about. Conigliaro became the youngest player to lead the American League in home runs, hitting 32 in his second year with the team.

But the day after Morehead's pitching gem, the Red Sox made the first move that was to bring the club back to glory. Owner Tom Yawkey fired Mike Higgins as general manager and brought in Dick O'Connell from his job as head of the Red Sox farm system. The progress would not be overnight, but the corner had been turned.

The team began to unload players who had gone past their prime. Bill Monbouquette, the hard-throwing righthander, had been a 20-game winner for Boston in 1963 and had hurled a no-hitter against Chicago in 1962. From nearby Medford, he was a hometown favorite, but he had fallen to 10-18 in 1965, so in October he was traded to Detroit.

Gone, too, was the folk hero of the Red Sox in the early 1960s, Dick Radatz. "The Monster" had been the best relief pitcher in the American League from 1962 through 1964; he was the scourge of the league, and managers told their teams that if they went into the final two innings against the Red Sox trailing by even a run, to forget it – Radataz would protect the lead. But the big fireballer had tried to change his style by coming up with a breaking pitch and had hurt his arm. By the time he realized what he had done, it was too late. He was traded early in 1966 to Cleveland.

But later in 1966 the Red Sox made a mistake in cleaning house, one that, had it not been made, might even have given them the 1967 World Series and perhaps enabled them to remain a contender in 1968. But Earl Wilson, the big hard-throwing right-handed pitcher, the second black to play for the Red Sox, fell out of favor. He had been 12-8 for Boston in 1962 and had thrown a no-hitter against the Los Angeles Angels in June of 1962. He was 11-16 in 1963, 11-12 in 1964, 13-14 in 1965. Even so, he was traded to the Detroit Tigers in 1966 for pitcher Julio Navarro and infielder Don Demeter. Neither ever amounted to much for Boston, whereas Wilson won 13 games for the Tigers in 1966, was 21-11 for them in 1967, 13-12 in 1968 and 12-10 in 1969.

If the Red Sox were changing in 1966, they didn't change their standing in the pennant race. They finished ninth again, saved from total ignominy by an even more inept New York Yankee team that was one game worse than Boston. Still, things continued to improve in small ways. There was, for example, a 26-year-old right-handed pitcher by the name of Jose Santiago who won 12 and lost 13 for the '66 team. Also, a big first baseman was brought up to the Red Sox, and he wowed everyone with his home run swing and his superb play at first. George Scott had a big gold tooth in front, a huge smile and a gift for gab. The fans loved this big guy from Greenville, Mississippi. George batted only .245 and struck out 154 times, but he knocked in 90 runs and hit 27 homers, and he augured well for the future.

The pieces were falling into place, with Scott at first and Rico Petrocelli in his second year at shortstop, with Carl Yastrzemski solid in left and Tony Conigliaro winning fans and the hearts of young women with his boyish good looks. And in addition to Santiago there was another young righthanded pitcher, Jim Lonborg, who had graduated from Stanford and had wanted to be a doctor or a dentist; he had won nine games in 1965, and in 1966 his record was 10-10. Having given up Radatz, the Red Sox hoped to help the bullpen by trading with Kansas City for John Wyatt, a chunky righthander who threw hard (and reportedly also threw a vaseline pitch). Wyatt came over to Boston with outfielder Jose Tartabull – a name that will long be remembered by true Red Sox fans.

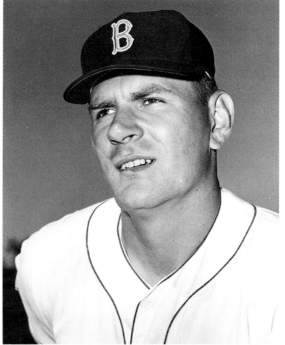

Far left: *In only his second season, Tony Conigliaro hit 32 homers to lead the American League in 1965. The outfielder became the youngest player ever to hit 100 home runs, before the tragic injury in 1967 that shortened his career.*

Left: *Hard-throwing reliever Dick Radatz was traded early in 1966 to Cleveland.*

The final move was to get the right manager. Billy Herman, who had managed from mid-1964, when Johnny Pesky was fired, was let go in the 1966 season, in which the Sox ended up 72-90. Pete Runnels was the interim manager to end the season, and then O'Connell dipped into the Red Sox farm system for Dick Williams, who had been managing the farm team at Toronto. In 1967 Williams arrived with a new get-tough policy, vowing that the so-called country-club atmosphere of the Red Sox clubhouse would be no more.

Williams was a stern disciplinarian, and he stressed fundamentals. He feuded with George Scott, saying he was too fat, and set limits for his weight; he benched Scott when he didn't reach the goals set for him. Williams made the whole team practice bunting, base running and hitting the cutoff-man on throws. And he ignored the team's gripes. "They probably thought I was crazy, but, hell, I had a one-year contract, so if I was crazy I was going to be crazy all year and give it the best I had. I didn't make too many friends among the players, but I don't care if they like me or not. I am concerned, though, about them respecting my knowledge of the game. If they do, they'll play for me, and they'll play at the top of their ability."

Williams arrived at spring training in 1967, along with most of the other pieces of the Impossible Dream puzzle. Among those pieces were a young second baseman, Mike Andrews and a shortstop, Reggie Smith, both of whom had played for Williams at Toronto in the International League. Now Williams needed to fit them and the other people into the right slots. Not too many people were convinced that he could suc-ceed, that he could change the attitude within the team known for years as "Yawkey's Millionaires" or that the people he had were really that good. Baltimore had won the pennant and the World Series the year before and remained a favorite this year, along with Detroit, which had Wilson and Denny McLain and Mickey Lolich. The Angels and the White Sox were also highly regarded.

Boston? Well, the oddsmakers in Las Vegas figured that Boston was a 100-1 shot, and there are no records of any New Englanders having put up $1000 on the Olde Towne Team to win that year. But Williams' miracle began early. He had Scott at first and was driving the Big Guy crazy with his criticism of his weight and his playing, but he was also driving him to a great season. Andrews took over as second baseman and played solid baseball, and Rico Petrocelli stayed at shortstop and hit 17 home runs and knocked in 66 runs while playing a strong defensive game. Joe Foy, who would eventually prove a disappointment as a major leaguer, was off to a good start for his former minor league manager as he drove in 49 runs and hit 16 homers while playing an aggressive third base.

The outfield was a gem. Carl Yastrzemski had come to the Red Sox hailed as a new Ted Williams. He wasn't, but he was a fine Carl Yastrzemski, and he had played for six years on bad teams and had hit .266, .296, .321 (to lead the league), .289, .312 and .278. He had a reputation of not giving it his all – played only as hard as he had to, as Manager Billy Herman had put it – but Yaz sensed something about this 1967 team, and he was off and running from the very start. Yaz would end with a league-leading

Jim Lonborg pitches his one-hit shutout in game two of the 1967 Series. On his way to a Cy Young Award that year, Lonborg won 22 games and lost just nine.

.326 average. He would also lead the league with 121 RBIs, and he shared the league lead in homers, with 44, tied with Harmon Killebrew of the Minnesota Twins. It was his Triple Crown year. In the field, Yaz was a phenom, catching impossible balls, making impossible throws and carrying the Red Sox to impossible heights.

Tony Conigliaro was a steady figure in right, playing solid defense and hitting in the clutch. Until his career-shattering injury late in the season, he was hitting .287, with 20 homers and 67 RBIs. The surprise was in center, where Reggie Smith was playing after Williams decided that Rico

should stay at shortstop. Smith was a defensive whiz, with great speed, and he hit .245, along with 15 homers and 61 RBIs. Meanwhile, Jim Lonborg and Jose Santiago were pitching up a storm and kept the Sox in the race from the start.

The Sox had many heroes that year. A game with the Chicago White Sox in June provides an example. It was a warm night at Fenway Park, and the two Sox teams were tied at 0-0 through the ninth. Lee Stange, a journeyman righthander was pitching for Boston. In the top of the 10th the White Sox scored a run and had runners on second and third with no outs, and Don

Buford was at the plate. The Red Sox played the infield in to cut off another run, and Scott crept to less than 50 feet from the plate to watch for a squeeze bunt. Instead, Buford swung away and rifled a shot toward right field. Scott dove with glove outstretched and caught the ball, got up and threw to third to double up the runner and snuff out the rally. In the last of the 10th, with one on and two out, Tony Conigliaro smashed a high fastball into the screen in left and gave the Red Sox a dramatic 2-1 win. Fans and the players were beginning to believe after games like that.

On June 3 there came another significant trade, this time with the White Sox, for a journeyman infielder named Jerry Adair who had never hit .300 – his last four years read .228, .248, .259, .249, hardly the stats of a pennant clincher. Adair came to Boston and quickly became Mr. Utility, filling in at third, at short and at second and hitting .271 and in the clutch. He provided the Red Sox with some infield depth and, although he was gone from Boston by 1969, Adair was to be a major contributor to the Impossible Dream.

But the baseball world was still not that convinced early on. Boston had a big road trip to the West coming up. The West had always been a graveyard for Red Sox teams, especially those accustomed to Fenway Park, with its Green Monster out in left for big righthanders to aim at. But the Sox came back from that road trip just three games out of first, and now people everywhere began to believe. The turnstiles spun, and Boston would go on to draw 1,727,000, a record at that time.

It became a four-way race: Boston, Detroit, Minnesota and California. The key

moments included a game in Chicago after the Red Sox lost the first game of a double-header and needed to win the second. Jose Tartabull, the throw-in on the John Wyatt deal, was in center, with Reggie Smith getting relief after the first game. The Red Sox led in the last of the ninth by a run. Ken Berry, a speedy outfielder, was on third for Chicago, with one out. A flyball was hit to medium center. Berry took off as Tartabull caught the ball and fired home. He wasn't noted for a strong arm, but the throw came in – too high! Elston Howard, the Red Sox catcher at that point, reached up for the throw and, blocking the plate with his leg, swept down and tagged Berry out. Boston had won. It was a key game, the kind that wins pennants, and Tartabull became a bit of Red Sox trivia.

The Red Sox continued to stay in the thick of things well into August, when the tragedy of August 18 unfolded. The Red Sox were at home to the Angels, and Tony Conigliaro was hitting in the eighth inning. Pitcher Jack Hamilton fired a high fastball inside. It was meant to drive Conigliaro back from the plate, but he froze, and the pitch crashed into his face, just beside his left eye. It fractured his cheekbone, dislocated his jaw and pushed part of his face into his eye. He lay on the ground at home plate, motionless, and the huge crowd in Fenway Park was eerily still until they finally carried Tony away to a hospital. He survived, but his promising baseball career was over.

The Red Sox kept on, despite the loss of their young slugger. They obtained Ken "The Hawk" Harrelson, a slugging out-fielder who had fallen out with Charley Finley, owner of the Kansas City team. Fin-

The talented 1967 Red Sox captured the American League crown under the helm of manager Dick Williams. The club went on to drop the World Series in seven games to Bob Gibson and the Cardinals.

ley had awarded Harrelson "free agency" long before it became a major part of baseball, and Boston signed him. Harrelson played 23 games for the Sox and helped keep them in the race.

It finally came down to the final series, two games with the Minnesota Twins at Fenway Park. The Twins led by a game. Boston had to sweep to come into first, and even then had to have Detroit lose one game against California to take sole possession of the pennant.

The Twins threw in their ace, Jim Kaat, the big lefthander, on Saturday. Boston countered with Jose Santiago. It was a tight game, and the Twins were leading when, in the seventh inning, Kaat pulled something in his arm. Boston went on to win 6-4. Boston was now tied with the Twins for the lead, with Detroit a half game back.

The next day it was Jim Lonborg, going for win No. 22, against Dean Chance, who was after No. 21. It was a tight game, but Lonborg started the winning rally with a bunt single. Then Lonborg withstood Killebrew's 44th home run to get the win with the final out of Rich Rollins, a popup that Rico Petrocelli caught. Final score, 5-3. Then the Red Sox waited out the California-Detroit game, and when the Angels won, Boston had its first pennant in 21 years. And as it had been in 1946, it was the Cardinals again providing the opposition in the World Series.

The key difference between the teams' readiness, beside the Sox having lost Conigliaro, was that the Sox had used Lonborg in the final game of the season. Bob Gibson of the Cardinals, meanwhile, had not worked since the previous Friday. Thus he could start the first game and conceivably pitch three times. Lonborg had to wait for Game 2, and though he could go twice, it was unlikely that he could be effective in three games.

It began true to form. Gibson won the first game 2-1 over Santiago, holding the Sox to six hits, including a home run by Santiago himself. Lonborg hurled a one-hit shutout in Game 2, also in Boston, with Julian Javier getting the lone Cardinal hit, while Yastrzemski hit two homers and knocked in three in the 5-0 victory.

At St. Louis, the Cards won 5-2, as Nelson Briles held Boston to seven hits, while Gary Bell and Gary Waslewski pitched for Boston. Mike Shannon's two-run homer was the key blow for St. Louis. Game 4 also went to St. Louis 6-0, as Gibson came back with a five-hitter and Santiago gave up four runs in the first. Game 5 was Lonborg's turn again, and he gave up only three hits and had a shutout until the ninth. Boston won 3-1, beating Steve Carl-

ton, a young Cardinal lefty in his second full season in the majors. Elston Howard singled in the winning run in the ninth.

Game 6 was back in Boston and became a key one, since neither Gibson nor Lonborg was available. This time Boston scored four in the seventh and held on for an 8-4 win, tying the Series at 3-3. Boston set a World Series record with three homers in the fourth by Petrocelli, Yastrzemski and Reggie Smith. Petrocelli hit a second homer, and the Cards tied a Series record by using eight pitchers in the game.

Game 7, the decider, was anticlimactic. Gibson was relatively rested, while Lonborg came back with just two days rest. The Cards struck for two runs in the third and rolled to a 7-2 win, with Gibson allowing only two hits. Gibson in fact gave up only 13 hits in his three games. Lou Brock had 12 hits in the Series, and Maris and Yaz both had 10.

As sad as the Series ending was for the

Red Sox and their fans, things looked fairly bright for 1968. Then came calamity. First it became clear that Conigliaro would not be back for 1968. Then it got worse when Lonborg went skiing during the winter, fell on a little jump and tore up his left knee. He was doubtful for 1968, maybe forever.

In fact, 1968 became a nightmare season. All the people – Adair, Wyatt, Gary Bell – who had added that little something extra in 1967 returned to their old form in 1968. Ken Harrelson had a good year, with 35 homers and 109 RBIs, but Boston finished at 86-76 (it had been 92-70 in 1967) and 17 in back of the Detroit Tigers, who took the pennant. The finishing blow was when Santiago tore a muscle in his pitching arm. It was surgically re-attached to the arm, but then it ripped loose again and his career ended.

The Red Sox had picked up two veteran National League pitchers in the off-season, and they were Boston's top winners in 1968: Dick Ellsworth, who came from the Phillies, and Ray Culp from the Cubs won 16 each for Boston. Culp was the leading winner in 1969, when Boston finished 87-75, 22 behind the champion Orioles. Lonborg did come back, but he was 6-10 in 1968 and 7-11 in 1969. Ellsworth was traded in 1969. George Scott went from his .303, 82 RBI, 19-homer season of 1967 to .171 in 1968 and .253 in 1969. Yaz dropped to .301 in 1968 and then to .255 in 1969.

Attendance averaged 1,900,000 in 1968 and 1969, but the honeymoon was clearly over, at least for the time being. Dick Williams was fired during the 1969 season, and coach Eddie Popowski took the team through the remainder of the games. Of course there was always hope of another miraculous turnaround, a new Impossible Dream, but it wasn't a very realistic hope. Indeed, the grim truth was that the Red Sox were about to enter possibly the most frustrating decade in the team's long history.

Elston Howard is too late on this tag at home against Paul Blair of the Baltimore Orioles in 1967. Howard was traded to the Red Sox from the Yankees during that season.

6. Near Misses

If the 1960s was the decade of the Impossible Dream, the 1970s was the decade of the recurrent nightmare. Not only did the Red Sox lose the World Series after taking the pennant (1975), but they missed their divisional crown four years by painfully narrow margins: a half game in 1972; by 7 in 1974, after they held a 7-game lead up to August 22; by 2½ games in 1977; by only one, and that after a playoff, in 1978. It must also be admitted that this decade saw the development of some of the superstars of Red Sox history – Fred Lynn, Jim Rice, Carlton Fisk and Dwight Evans, among others. But the '70s was also the decade of four ill-advised trades that would haunt the Sox for years.

The decade began with a new manager and a blockbuster deal that was the first of the bad ones for Boston. After the firing of

Tony Conigliaro considered making a comeback as a pitcher following his 1967 beaning. The Red Sox outfielder missed the 1968 season prior to his return in 1969.

Dick Williams near the end of the '69 season, General Manager Dick O'Connell reached down into the farm system again for a replacement and came up with Eddie Kasko, who had managed the Red Sox AAA farm team at Louisville to a second-place finish in 1969. Eddie had been an infielder for the Cardinals, Reds, Astros and Red Sox for 10 years (and would eventually become the scouting director for Boston).

Eddie took over a team in transition in 1970. Its leading pitcher was Ray Culp, with 17 wins. Jim Lonborg, the superstar of 1967, still was not back in form and went 4-1. Carl Yastrzemski led the team and the American League, with a .329 average, and Tony Conigliaro appeared to have recovered from the horrible beaning of 1967, hitting .266, with 36 home runs and 116 RBIs. Reggie Smith hit .303, and George

Scott had a banner year at .296, with 16 homers and 63 RBIs. The Sox won 87 games in 1970 but finished third in the AL East, 21 back of the rampaging Baltimore Orioles, who won 108 games and then went on to defeat the Cincinnati Reds in the World Series, four games to one.

In 1971, the second year of Kasko's management, the Red Sox won 85 games, leaving them 16 behind the AL East winners, again the Orioles, with 101 wins. The Sox did not have a .300 hitter in 1971, Reggie Smith's .283 being their best. Tony Conigliaro, his health still in question, had been traded the previous October to California for reliever Ken Tatum and rookie infielder Doug Griffin. Conigliaro played in 74 games for the Angels in 1971 but then had to give up baseball, his sight having deteriorated greatly. Tatum was 2-4 with the Red Sox, and Griffin batted a season .244, while becoming the regular second baseman.

Highlights of an otherwise forgettable season included the late arrival of a big catcher from Bellows Falls, Vermont, Carlton Fisk, who got into 14 games for the 1971 Sox and hit two home runs. Making a bigger splash was a utility fielder who had been acquired in 1970 from the Yankees but came into his own in 1971: John Kennedy hit .272, with five homers and 22 RBIs, and was nicknamed "Super Sub" because it seemed that every time he was called on in a clutch situation he came through with flying colors.

Another bright spot for the Sox in '71 was Jim Lonborg's winning 10 games (and losing 7). But Sonny Siebert, a pitcher acquired in a deal with Cleveland in 1969, was the top hurler for Boston, winning 16 games. A feisty lefthanded reliever, Albert Walter "Sparky" Lyle was 6-4, with 16 saves and a 2.77 ERA.

After the 1971 season the Red Sox management decided on drastic changes. First there was a huge deal with Milwaukee. George Scott, now out of favor with the Red Sox management, was packaged with Billy Conigliaro (Tony's younger brother), outfielders Joe Lahoud and Don Pavletich, pitchers Ken Brett (George's older brother) and Jim Lonborg and exchanged for pitchers Marty Pattin and Lew Krausse and outfielders Tommy Harper and Pat Skrable. It was a stunning deal and, as it turned out, a bad one for Boston. Lonborg won 14 games for Milwaukee in 1972, with a 2.83 ERA, and later was traded to Philadelphia, where he won 13, 17, 18, 8 and 11 games during five seasons. Scott batted .263, .266, .306, .281 and .285 in his five years with the Brewers, driving in 88, 107, 82, 109 and 77 runs during those same

years and clouting an average of 23 homers a season, with 36 in 1975 alone. Meanwhile, although Pattin was 17-13 for Boston in 1972 and 15-15 in 1973, he was then traded away. Harper batted .254 and .281 in his two years with the Sox before being traded. It was a case of the Red Sox deciding to clean house too thoroughly by half.

But as bad as that trade was, the one consummated just before the 1972 season began was worse, both for 1972 and for many years to come. Kasko and the Red Sox were concerned with what to do about first base after the departure of George Scott, but nobody seemed to think there was any need to worry about the bullpen. Indeed, they worried so little that on March 22, just two weeks before the season began, Sparky Lyle was sent to the New York Yankees for first baseman Danny Cater. Cater had hit well at Fenway Park when he played for the Chicago White Sox in 1965, the Kansas City A's in 1967-69 and the Yankees in 1970-71, so he seemed like a good choice.

Red Sox catcher Carlton Fisk was the American League's Rookie of the Year in 1972. Fisk, who hit 22 homers and batted .293 that year, played in Boston until 1981.

In his 19-year career, Luis Tiant posted four 20-win seasons. Tiant won 20 games three times for the Red Sox after joining the club in 1971.

But Cater hit only .273 for the Red Sox in 1972, and in 1975 he was traded to St. Louis. Lyle, meanwhile, was 9-5 for New York in 1972 and for six years reigned as one of the top relievers in baseball.

Despite all this, the Red Sox came oh-so-close in 1972, done in by a strike-shortened season and a pair of falls by a future Hall of Famer. The short-lived players' strike at the start of the season cost the Red Sox seven games off their schedule, but it cost the Tigers only six games, and Detroit ended up winning the division by a half game, 86-70 to Boston's 85-70. It was a strange season for Boston in other ways because of the trades and the lack of any .300 hitter; Pudge Fisk, the catcher, came closest, at .293. Boston fans also cheered the base-stealing skills of Tommy Harper, who played center and hit .254, while stealing 25 bases. The fans also came out, 1,441,000-strong, to boo Carl Yastrzemski. He had signed a three-year contract at the then unheard-of salary of $500,000 for three years, and fans both resented the amount and hooted because Yaz had only good years, not great ones.

Still, the Sox got down to the end of the 1972 season in good shape. They beat Milwaukee on September 27, then took Kansas City on September 28 and led by a game and a half. They then went into Baltimore, and Luis Tiant won on September 29, his 15th win of the season. Mart Pattin won his 16th on September 30, and Boston held its 1½-game lead, even though the Tigers were also winning. On October 1, a Sunday, Lynn McGlothen, a hardthrowing righthander, lost a heartbreaker at Baltimore to the Orioles' Mike Cuellar, who won his 18th game 2-1. Boston now headed for Detroit, up by only a half game and needing to win two of the three final games of the season.

The key game was the opener. John Curtis, a young lefty, went for Boston against the Tigers' Mickey Lolich, going for win No. 22. It was said of Lolich that if you couldn't get him in the early innings, he would surely beat you. Boston tried. After the Sox scored one run Luis Aparicio got on first with one out. There was a drive into the gap, and Aparicio came around third base and started for home and the second run of the inning. But, just past third, Aparicio tripped on his own feet and fell. He tried to crawl back to third, but it was too late. The throw got him, the rally fizzled and Lolich, who had appeared to be on the ropes, finished out a 4-1 victory. Curiously, early in the season Aparacio had also fallen while rounding third and had failed to score, thus costing Boston a game – also against Detroit.

The Sox now trailed by a half game and had to win on Tuesday to have a shot at the AL East title. But Tiant lost a 3-1 pitching duel with veteran National League castoff Woody Fryman, who had already won nine games for Detroit that season. Boston won the final game of the season, but it was academic. The Red Sox and their fans then had to watch Oakland beat the Tigers for the AL pennant and go on to beat Cincinnati in the 1972 World Series.

Sox fans were stunned, but at least they still had Yaz to boo and Fisk to cheer. They also had a rising new star. The Sox had traded Mike Andrews and shortstop Luis Alvarado to Chicago for Aparicio at the end of the 1970 season, and about the same time they had picked up another Latin player for nothing: Luis Tiant. He had been a 20-game winner for Cleveland in 1968, but after five winning seasons with the Indians the Cuban-born righthander had suffered arm problems and had drifted off to Minnesota, then to Richmond in the minors and then to release. Boston's manager at the Louisville farm club, Darrell Johnson, suggested it might be worth signing Tiant to a minor league contract and see if he could pitch again. Johnson got the go-ahead, watched Tiant go 4-2 and recommended that the Sox bring him up. They did, and though Tiant was only 1-7 for the rest of 1971, he looked as if he could pitch. His motion was interesting, his fastball was live and the fans liked him. Before long they would love him.

Aparicio hit .237 for Boston in 1971, .257 in 1972 and .271 in 1973, then retired after the 1973 season. But Tiant was just getting started. He was 15-6 with Boston in 1972, with a sizzling 1.91 ERA. The fans delighted in his pitching style. With his arms ex-

Below: *The plaque commemorating Luis Aparicio at the Hall of Fame, to which he was elected in 1984. The slick-fielding shortstop won nine Gold Glove Awards in 18 big league seasons.*

tended high overhead and then brought down in short jerky motions until they came to his belt buckle, he would swing around to face centerfield, then suddenly whirl and deliver the pitch to the plate. It drove opposing hitters wild to see this man who threw a 90-mile-an-hour fastball not even looking at the batter until he let the ball go.

There were more changes in store for

Above: *Luis Aparicio closed out his career as Boston's regular shortstop. His best season for the Red Sox was 1973, when he batted .271.*

LUIS ERNESTO APARICIO

CHICAGO A.L. 1956-1962, 1968-1970
BALTIMORE A.L. 1963-1967
BOSTON A.L. 1971-1973

REGULAR SHORTSTOP FOR ALL OF HIS 18 SEASONS. SET MAJOR LEAGUE CAREER RECORDS FOR MOST GAMES (2,581), ASSISTS (8,016), CHANCES ACCEPTED (12,564) AND DOUBLE PLAYS (1,553) BY A SHORTSTOP; AND HAS MOST A.L. PUTOUTS (4,548). LED A.L. IN FIELDING 8 TIMES. TOPPED LEAGUE IN STEALS HIS FIRST 9 SEASONS, BEGINNING STOLEN BASE RENAISSANCE. A.L. ROOKIE OF THE YEAR IN 1956.

Like father, like son! Two-year-old Casey Fisk enjoys a lollipop as his dad Carlton holds the youngster's plastic bat in the very first Red Sox Son and Daughter baseball game, in June of 1974.

Boston in 1973, but they didn't bring a pennant. Boston went 89-73, but Baltimore went 97-65 to win by eight games – only to lose to Oakland in the playoffs. (The A's then beat the Mets in the World Series 4-3.) The Sox were paced in 1973 by Reggie Smith's .303 season, with 21 homers and 60 RBIs, while Yaz hit .296, with 19 homers and 95 RBIs and lots of boos. Harper now played left, and Rick Miller, who had played in 89 games (92 at bats) in 1972, was now in center. Fisk dropped to .246, and the Sox obtained former St. Louis and San Francisco slugger Orlando Cepeda to be designated hitter for the first year of this new rule. Cepeda hit .289, with 20 homers and 86 RBIs. And there was also a rookie who had come up late in the season, Dwight Evans, who showed great promise.

Tiant won 20 games in 1973, the first Red Sox pitcher to do that since Lonborg in 1967, and Bill Lee, in his third full season, won 17. The bullpen was manned by veterans Bob Bolin (15 saves) and Bob Veale (11 saves). Lyle, meanwhile, had 27 saves and a 2.51 ERA for the Yankees.

In the off-season the Red Sox made some key moves. Eddie Kasko was fired as manager and became a team scout. Darrell Johnson became the team's 30th manager after his two years at Louisville. He had led the Sox top farm team to a pennant in 1972, and the next year he led it to the Junior World Series championship.

It was also decided that something had to be done about the element that the Red Sox had been missing for years – pitching. With Rick Miller apparently ready to be the regular centerfielder, the Red Sox worked a major trade with the St. Louis Cardinals, sending off Reggie Smith and pitcher Ken Tatum for Rick Wise and Bernie Carbo, an outfielder. Wise had won 16 games each of the previous two years for St. Louis and was a hardthrowing righthander; Carbo was a lefthanded outfielder with power. Tatum had not proved a success with the Red Sox since he came over from California in 1971, and Reggie Smith, who hit .303 in 1971, had been feuding with the Sox management and the Boston media. The deal seemed to satisfy all the needs.

Six weeks later, on December 7, 1973, the Sox closed a second deal with the Cardinals, sending pitchers John Curtis (13-13 in '73), Mike Garman (0-0 in '73), and Lynn McGlothen (1-2 in '73) for Reggie Cleveland, a righthander who had won 14 and lost 10 for the Cards in 1973, and for reliever Diego Segui, 7-6, with a 2.81 ERA at St. Louis in 1973.

But two calamities befell the Red Sox in 1974, and they would work to make the year a disappointing one and let the team get the nickname of "chokers." First Fisk, who appeared to be ready for greatness, tore up his left knee while blocking the plate in a June 28 game at Cleveland. He had surgery and was out for the rest of the season. Catching, meant to be a Sox strongpoint, became a weak one instead. Then Wise, who was expected to join with Luis Tiant and Bill Lee to give the Sox a solid 1-2-3 punch on the mound, missed much of the early part of the season with a shoulder injury, and when he was coming back from that he broke a finger when his wife accidentally closed a door on his hand. He ended up at 3-4 with Boston in 1974.

But the team persevered, actually holding a seven-game lead as of August 21. Then the Sox went into an incredible slump, losing 24 of the final 38 games and dropping all the way to third. Boston fans were livid, and some said that the Sox had been playing over their heads all along and

that it had finally caught up with them, especially when they lacked Fisk and Wise.

Baltimore easily won the AL East in 1974, then lost to Oakland for the third consecutive time, and the A's went on to beat the L.A. Dodgers 4-1 for a third straight championship. Boston licked its wounds, taking some consolation from Yaz's .301 average, with 15 homers and 79 RBIs. Dwight Evans had .281, 10 homers and 70 RBIs. And there were 22 wins for Tiant and 17 for Bill Lee. Twice in three years now, the Red Sox fans had thought they had the pennant, and twice the team had failed them. It appeared that in 1975 the Sox might have a hard time keeping the fans coming. But with Fred Lynn and Jim Rice due on the scene, no one need have worried.

When the new designated hitter rule was put into place in 1972, the Red Sox went out and obtained the services of Orlando Cepeda. The former National League slugger hit 20 homers.

7. The Glories of '75

The 1975 baseball season should have dawned for Red Sox fans with bright hopes. After all, the team had made a legitimate run for the pennant the previous year, and this time the team would have Pudge Fisk and Rick Wise for full seasons. Rick Burleson had surprised everyone by playing outstanding shortstop and hitting higher in the majors than he ever had in the minors. In addition, there were the two rookies who gave every indication they would be phenoms, Fred Lynn and Jim Rice. But the memory of the collapse of 1974 still hung heavy over New England fans.

At first most of the pre-season talk had to do with the decision by Tony Conigliaro to try one more comeback and with the salary hassle concerning Luis Tiant, who felt he deserved more than the $70,000 he was earning and wouldn't show up at Winter Haven, Florida, causing team owner Tom Yawkey to meet with El Tiante, agree on a raise (to $90,000) and get the Sox pitching ace back in camp.

Still, it didn't take too long before the stories and pictures coming out of Florida about the two phenoms got Sox fans thinking. The gamblers in Vegas had Boston as a long shot, although not the 100-1 shot they were in '67. The odds against them went up, however, after Fisk, returning from the serious knee injury of 1974, was hit in the right arm and broke it. Even the positive talk about young Mr. Lynn couldn't drive away the gloom over Fisk's injury. Catching is absolutely vital to a successful team, and Fisk was going to be sidelined for at least a couple of months.

Yet the word out of Florida on Lynn *was* pretty positive. The young man who had gone to Southern California as a football linebacker, but gave up football for baseball, seemed to be doing it all. Not only did he hit and run and field, he was a good-looking, charming young man. He would be a hit with Boston and New England fans, no question. What's more, he was hitting with power, and with the way big Jim Rice was

Far right: *Fred Lynn takes a lead off the base. The promising outfielder led the league in doubles, runs, and slugging average in 1975 – a performance that earned him Rookie of the Year and Most Valuable Player honors.*

Right: *Jim Rice, who was injured late in the season, also had fine rookie campaign, with 22 homers and 102 runs batted in.*

clobbering the baseball, Boston appeared to have a real power punch that could only get better when Fisk got back into the lineup.

Rick Wise, back after a year of shoulder trouble and then a broken finger, looked ready to boost the pitching staff, which already had Luis Tiant, Bill Lee, Reggie Cleveland and the stringbean flame-thrower Roger Moret. The bullpen also looked strong, with Dick Drago as the closer and hard-thrower Dick Pole and veteran Diego Segui.

Additionally, the word on Tony C was encouraging, and that boosted spirits back home. Yaz would be playing first, and after three short trials in previous years Cecil Cooper was going to make this team and probably be the designated hitter.

The season opened with El Tiante beating the Milwaukee Brewers, and after the first week the Sox shared first with Milwaukee. Rice was playing some left field, and his defense left a lot to be desired; people already were saying that Rice might be a one-dimensional player who had to be the designated hitter only. On the other hand, Lynn was doing well, and the problems at catcher were not apparent yet.

The Red Sox fell out of first place in late April and didn't get back into it until the end of May. Lynn was bombing American League pitching and playing great center-field, and Rice was clobbering the ball. But the Red Sox were winning a lot of high-scoring games which didn't augur well for pitching when the pennant race reached the dog days of August and September.

In June the Red Sox made what appeared to be a minor move to bolster the bench when they bought journeyman second baseman Denny Doyle from the California Angels. The Angels would get cash and a player to be named later, the quality depending on what Doyle did for the Sox. Little did anyone know this would be even better than the pickup of Jerry Adair back in 1967.

Second base was a Sox problem. Doug Griffin was playing there and doing an adequate job, but he was injury-prone, and the Sox had been particularly anxious about him ever since he had been hit in the face by a Nolan Ryan fastball back in April of 1974. Doug had seemed tentative at the plate since the beaning, and Boston had concerns about his durability and about his ability to stand in there on inside pitches.

Doyle arrived on June 14, and to make room for him on the roster Tony Conigliaro was sent to Pawtucket in the minor leagues. Tony's attempt to come back hadn't really worked out. On his first at-bat he homered for the Sox, but soon thereafter it became apparent that the eye damage had been too great and that the once-promising career now was over for good.

Rick Burleson was a key member of the Red Sox for seven years. A slick-fielding shortstop, "Rooster" left Boston for the California Angels in 1981.

Right: *With a spectacular diving catch, stellar outfielder Fred Lynn robs the Reds' Dave Concepcion in game two of the 1975 World Series.*

Opposite: *Luis Tiant won two games in the 1975 World Series. The Red Sox ace also collected a three-hit victory against Oakland in the American League Championship Series.*

So the Red Sox got Denny Doyle into the lineup, and no one could get him out of it for the rest of the season. He ended up hitting .310, had a 22-game hitting streak and was outstanding in the field. In fact, he cemented an infield which featured Yaz at first, Burleson at short and Rico Petrocelli at third. A major step toward the pennant had been taken with the Doyle deal.

On June 18 Fred Lynn had one of those games that players can only dream about. The Red Sox were in Detroit and had won the first two games of the series, with second-year regular Juan Beniquez having two big games – a triple to start a winning rally in the opener and a homer to win the second. Unable to sleep, Fred Lynn got up, got dressed and walked the streets of downtown Detroit for an hour or two after 6 a.m. Still restless, he had breakfast and then went to Tiger Stadium to get extra batting practice. Whatever it was in the recipe that worked, it worked remarkably well.

In the four-run first inning he crashed a homer into the upper deck in right. In the three-run second he clubbed one off the roof of the upper deck in left center. In the third he just missed when his long drive to left center hit the top of the fence and came back for a triple. In the sixth he beat out an infield single, and then in the ninth he smashed a three-run homer to the upper deck in right again. Lynn had hit his 12th, 13th and 14th home runs, had knocked in 10 runs, tying the Red Sox record for RBIs in a game, and Luis Tiant had no trouble winning his ninth game, 15-1.

The Sox went in and out of first place three different times in late June, but at the end of the month they led the Yankees by a game. Baltimore was 7½ back, five games under .500.

In early July the Red Sox put Jim Rice into left field. Since Carlton Fisk had returned a week earlier, the Sox now had a power-laden lineup that was the talk of baseball. But Baltimore was getting ready to make a move, looking for a third consecutive division crown. And after the Orioles clobbered Boston on July 1, 10-6, Oriole manager Earl Weaver suggested that whereas his team would emulate the 1974 Oriole club, picking up a game a week, Boston would emulate its 1974 team and fade. It made for good reading.

Rice broke in as a regular with two homers in a 6-3 win at Milwaukee, in which Wise had a no-hitter through 8⅔ innings but lost it when George Scott homered in the ninth. The Red Sox completed a sweep of the Twins in Minnesota and did the same to the Rangers in Texas, and by All-Star break they held a 4½ game lead over the Yankees and Brewers.

The Sox then put together a 10-game winning streak, moved six ahead of the Yankees and finally put the Yankees away with a three-out-of-four series victory in New York, featuring two shutouts pitched by lefthanders, on Sunday, July 27. Bill Lee beat Catfish Hunter in the first 1-0, with Lynn making one of the great catches in baseball history as he ran into left-center field and dived for a drive hit by Graig Nettles. He caught the ball in his glove and, when he hit the ground, the ball popped out of the glove. He simply reached up and grabbed it before it hit the ground.

Roger Moret pitched his seventh win, against one loss, in a 6-0 Boston win in the nightcap, featuring Yaz's 12th home run. By the end of July Boston enjoyed an eight-game lead over the Orioles, who had moved to 51-47, over .500 for the first time.

A wistful Jim Rice in the dugout at Cincinnati before the fourth game of the 1975 World Series. Rice, who suffered a broken bone in the left hand when struck by a pitch late in September, could only watch as the Sox took the field for post-season play.

The lead got to 9½ games and then began to dwindle down to six by September 1. But there was no question that the fans now believed: the crowds filled Fenway. Boston next took two from the Orioles at Baltimore. Weaver was subdued, and Boston led by seven. By September 15 the Sox had not collapsed as they had in 1974, but the lead over the Orioles was down to four. The game that may have decided the season was played on Tuesday, September 16, at hot, humid and jammed Fenway. Luis Tiant against Jim Palmer.

The crowd chanted "Loo-eee! Loo-eee! Loo-eee!," and he responded, twirling, looking into center and then blowing the ball by the Orioles. Palmer was good, but Loo-eee! was better. Boston won 2-0 on homers by Fisk and Petrocelli.

It stayed close until Friday, September 26. It had rained for five days. Contingency plans to make up rained-out games had been made, but it became academic on Friday, for the rain had stopped. But the field at Fenway was soggy, and there was a lot of fog. Nevertheless, they played a twi-night doubleheader with Cleveland. Tiant won the opener 4-0, besting Dennis Eckersley in a game in which part of left field was in fog.

Reggie Cleveland won the second game, also 4-0, and the Sox had clinched a tie for first. The next day the Yankees finished off the Orioles, winning a twin bill at New York. Boston was thus the AL East champ, and Oakland was their next obstacle on the way to the World Series.

The only negative part was that Rice had broken a bone in his left hand when struck by a pitch from the Tigers' Vern Ruhle and would be out for the rest of the season. So for the playoffs Manager Darrell Johnson had to do some juggling, putting Yaz back in left. One of the best defensive left fielders ever at Boston, Yaz had been moved to first to prolong his career. But now he was back in left, and Cooper was going to first.

Oakland was favored, but that was to be expected. The A's were trying to become the only other team to win four consecutive World Series. (The Yankees had done it a couple of times.)

But it wasn't even close. At Fenway Park, in Game 1 of the best-of-five series, Luis Tiant twirled a three-hitter, the Oaklands made four errors and the Sox won, 7-1, as Lynn doubled home two runs in Boston's five-run seventh.

Game 2 in Boston saw Rico Petrocelli homer and Yaz blast a two-run home run. Though Reggie Jackson hit one with one on for Oakland, Boston won 6-3, after spotting the A's two on Jackson's homer in the first. Cleveland was the winning pitcher, with Moret and Drago in relief.

Owner Tom Yawkey shut down Fenway Park and took every Sox employee to Oakland for Game 3 on Oct. 7, and this time Rick Wise was the winner, 5-3, with Drago getting the save. Yaz, playing like a kid again, had two hits and made two great catches to stop the A's. So it was on to the World Series and the Big Red Machine from Cincinnati.

This has been called by some the best World Series ever. That's a subjective view, open to argument, but no one will question that Game 6 was one of the most exciting baseball games ever played, perhaps *the* most exciting.

The Series started like the league playoffs, as Tiant threw a five-hitter and even singled and scored the first run (no designated hitters in the World Series). Boston won, 6-0, over Don Gullett, who had held Boston scoreless until the seventh, when the Sox unloaded all six runs.

Game 2 saw the Sox and Bill Lee leading 2-1 going into the ninth, when there was a rain delay. When play resumed Lee had cooled off and the Reds rallied, with Johnny Bench doubling off Lee. After Dick Drago, in relief, got two outs, he gave up a single to Dave Concepcion that tied the game. Dave stole second and then came home with the winning run on a single by Ken Griffey.

Game 3 was a hotly disputed contest, with the Reds winning 6-5 in 10 innings. Evans had tied the game at 5-5 with a two-run homer in the ninth, and, with no one out in the 10th, Cesar Geronimo had singled off reliever Jim Willoughby. Ed Armbrister then bunted, and when Fisk went to field the ball to throw to second, he and Armbrister collided. Fisk threw late and wild to second, and Geronimo went to third. Though Fisk and the Sox screamed it was interference, American League umpire Larry Barnett said it was not. The next batter lifted a long fly to center, and that brought in the winning run.

Irate, the Sox game came back to win Game 4 by a score of 5-4, with Luis Tiant winning despite throwing 163 pitches. Boston scored five in the third for the win.

Game 5 was the Reds all the way, as they clubbed Reggie Cleveland and Dick Pole, with Tony Perez hitting two homers, one with two on. Gullett was the winner.

Game 6 was one for posterity. Rain delayed the game three days, and then it was Tiant against Gary Nolan at Fenway Park. The Sox broke out with three in the first inning on Lynn's home run, but the Reds tied in the fifth and then seemed to have the Series well in hand, with two in the seventh and one in the eighth. Then came the heroics.

In the last of the eighth the Sox got two on against reliever Pedro Borbon. Cincinnati Manager Sparky Anderson brought in his top reliever, Rawley Eastwick, who had two wins in the series. He struck out Evans and got Burleson on a short fly ball. Bernie Carbo, a former Red, was sent up to pinch hit. The count went to two and two, and Carbo had looked very bad on the second strike. Carbo said he was just trying to foul the pitch off, but on 2-2 he was ready. Eastwick got the ball up, and Carbo crashed it to center. Geronimo went back for it, but it carried into the bleachers. The game was tied.

The Sox had the bases loaded in the ninth, with no outs, but they couldn't score. In the 11th the Reds had a runner on first, with one out, when Joe Morgan hit a long drive to right. Evans went back and made a great catch at the fence and then threw in to double the runner. Finally, at 12:30 in the morning in the last of the 12th, Fisk greeted the Reds' eighth pitcher of the game, Pat Darcy, with a drive down the left-field line. Fisk stood midway between the plate and first and, waving his hands, trying to will the ball to be fair. It hit the foul pole, a home run, and Boston had pulled it out. It was a game that Pete Rose said should be shown all over the world to build fans for baseball.

Game 7 was almost anticlimactic. Boston took a 3-0 lead in the third on a Lynn homer. Perez then brought the Reds back

with a two-run blast in the sixth when Bill Lee threw Tony his eephus pitch, a rainbow-like slowball that had gotten the slugger three other times in the Series, but not this time. The Reds tied with a run in the eighth and won on a looping single to center by Joe Morgan off reliever Jim Burton. Thus the Reds won the Series 4-3. Pete Rose was the Series MVP, with a .370 average. Yaz topped all the Red Sox hitters at .311. Lynn was named AL MVP and co-rookie of the year along with Jim Rice.

Boston fans were both proud and disappointed, and they were more than ever impatient for the next season to begin.

Top: *Luis Tiant is safe at second base in the opening game of the 1975 World Series. Luis went on to score, and to shut out the Reds, 6-0.*

Above: *Carlton Fisk and Ed Armbrister of the Reds were the center of controversy in game three of the 1975 classic.*

8. More Hopes Dashed

If ever a team looked golden for a second pennant the 1976 Red Sox were the ones. The team that had celebrated the 75th anniversary of the Boston Red Sox in 1975 was healthy, appeared stronger and more experienced, and, although Dick Drago had been traded to California (to complete the deal for Denny Doyle), the team had picked up veteran righthander Ferguson Jenkins. The acquisition of Jim Willoughby from the St. Louis Cardinals farm system in mid-1975 had also solidified the bullpen, so that even the loss of Drago didn't appear to be a calamity.

But pennants aren't won on paper, and there were some serious problems with the Red Sox. They began to appear as spring training got under way.

The Andy Messersmith-Dave McNally decision haunted the Red Sox in 1976. After an arbitrator had ruled in 1975 that a team did not have permanent rights to a player, all of baseball was trying to come to grips with the new management-player relationship, but it hurt the Red Sox and the Oakland Athletics more than anyone.

In particular, Fisk, Lynn and Burleson wanted big pay hikes, and they held out, disrupting spring training and the team's solidarity. They were the "reluctant trio," and the fans who had cheered them the year before were reviling them in 1976 as they played and griped and negotiated.

Any chance of resolving the matter amicably went out the window with the death in July of Tom Yawkey. He had owned the Red Sox for 44 years, the longest any major league team had been owned by one individual. Yawkey had taken the Red Sox from the depths of despair in 1932 and had brought them back to respectability. He had seen them win three pennants and lose three World Series, but always entertain. His fight with leukemia had been kept a secret, and it is felt that if he had been healthy he would amost certainly have settled the "reluctant trio" situation early and that the '76 season might have been different from what it was.

With Yawkey gone there was a kind of power vacuum, the contract talks dragged on, and the team was rent with dissension. Lynn, who had been hailed as the conquering hero in 1975, admitted that the boos he received at Fenway the next year were hard to take. He and Fisk and Burleson became increasingly restless and bitter, and that would play a big role in their eventual departure from Fenway Park four years later.

Whatever the reasons, the Sox struggled to a third-place finish behind the champion Yankees and the Orioles. In 1975 Boston had gone 95-65. Now they finished 83-79, costing Darrell Johnson his job as manager. He was replaced in July by Don Zimmer, the third base coach.

Luis Tiant had another big year, celebrating the arrival, late in the 1975 season, of his parents from Cuba, their passage to the U.S. helped by Senator Edward Brooke of Massachusetts and Tom Yawkey. The

Ferguson Jenkins joined the Red Sox' pitching corp in 1976 and won 12 games. Boston did not do well, however, finishing 16 games under .500.

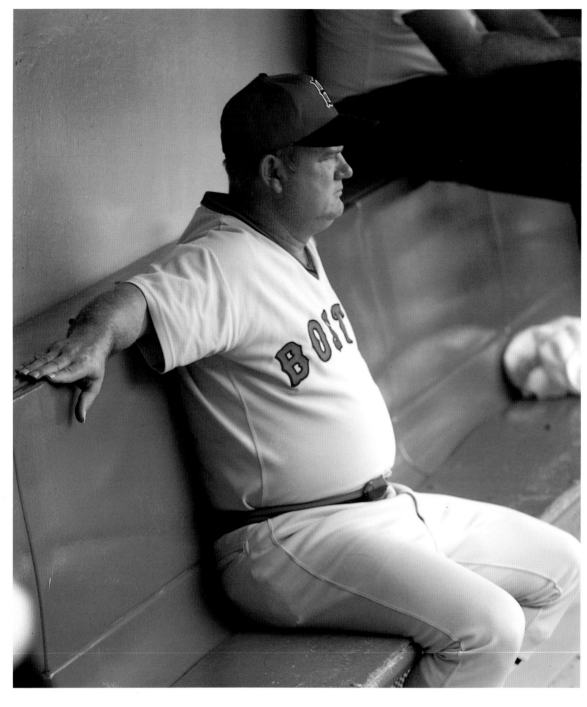

Don Zimmer was called on to manage the Red Sox in July of 1976. Zimmer took a seat in the dugout after coaching third base for Darrell Johnson.

parents moved permanently to Boston, and watched Luis pick up 21 wins in 1976. However, Rick Wise fell from 19 wins in 1975 to 14 in 1976, and while Ferguson Jenkins scored 12 wins, Reggie Cleveland dropped from 14 to 10, and Bill Lee from 17 to five.

Don Zimmer believed in big guys who could take advantage of the left field fence at Fenway. In addition, he hadn't been fond of Cecil Cooper since Cooper's sub-par 1975 World Series. Cooper hit .282, with 15 homers and 78 RBIs, in 1976, but Zimmer wanted to trade him. When the Milwaukee Brewers indicated a willingness to trade George Scott for Cooper, Zimmer was in favor. General Manager Dick O'Connell was hesitant, yet he didn't want to go against the man picked to manage the team. Instead, all the team's coaches and scouts were polled. The vote was 10-1

against the trade. But the one was Zimmer.

Reluctantly O'Connell agreed to the deal. Cooper was 27 years old, Scott 33. Scott had, to be sure, a good year in 1977, batted .269, hit 33 homers and drove in 95 runs. But Cooper, who had never hit under .300 in the Red Sox farm system, hit .300, with 20 homers and 78 RBIs, for the Brewers in 1977.

Throughout much of 1977 the future of the team's ownership was unclear. There were several syndicates bidding for the team, which eventually in 1977 went to one headed by Haywood Sullivan, the vice president in charge of player personnel. Another of the majority partners was former Red Sox trainer Edward "Buddy" LeRoux, and the third was Mrs. Yawkey, who put up Fenway Park as collateral in the $15 million deal. (Today the Red Sox franchise is considered to be worth $60 million or more.) Sullivan became president, LeRoux a vice president and Mrs. Yawkey a majority partner, but with no title, although her representative, John Harrington, was treasurer.

The team dipped into the free agent market in that first year of the market's existence and got Minnesota's ace reliever Bill Campbell. The price was $1 million for three years. The era of the big money players had begun.

Otherwise, 1977 was another of those seasons in which Red Sox fans were given high hopes, only to have them dashed. Denny Doyle dropped to .240, Evans to .230 and Lynn to .260, with 18 homers and 76 RBIs. Tiant slipped to 12-8, Fergy Jenkins won only 10 and Wise 11. A rookie named Bob Stanley came up and won 8 games. Campbell paid dividends, being used again and again out of the bullpen and winning 13 games and losing 9 and, with 31 saves. Many thought he was being used too much.

Despite it all, the Sox were in the pennant race until the last weekend, when they had a series with Baltimore, with both teams having a shot at the Yankees. One or the other had to sweep the other, but neither did, and the Red Sox won 97 games and finished tied with Baltimore, 2 games back of New York, which beat Los Angeles in the World Series that year.

It is possible that one of the last deals

Right: *Starter Reggie Cleveland won 11 games and lost eight in 1977 for the Red Sox. Cleveland posted an earned run average of 4.26 and had nine complete games in 36 appearances.*

that Tom Yawkey tried to make in 1976 might have made a big difference for the Red Sox in 1977 and 1978. Yawkey had been prepared to buy Joe Rudi and Rollie Fingers from the Oakland A's for $1 million each. At the same time the Yankees were preparing to buy Vida Blue from the A's for the same amount. Charlie Finley of the A's obviously needed money. But Commissioner Bowie Kuhn, not a Finley friend, stepped in and banned the sales as being detrimental to baseball. Many Boston fans wondered why Commissioner Landis had not done the same back in 1920, when Harry Frazee sold Babe Ruth and so many others to the Yankees. In any case the Sox entered 1977 without Rudi and Fingers and fell short.

If the fans had experienced a letdown in 1977, 1978 was infinitely worse. During the off-season the Sox went to the free agent market and got Mike Torrez, hero of the 1977 World Series for the Yankees, bringing him to Boston for five years for $2.9 million. Then the final piece of the puzzle seemed to have been put into place when the Sox and Cleveland Indians worked out

a major deal during March. The Sox traded rookie infielder Ted Cox, second-year pitcher Mike Paxton, Rick Wise and catcher Bo Diaz for Cleveland's right-handed ace, Dennis Eckersley. The hard-throwing Eckersley seemed to be all that the Sox needed, given a power-laden lineup that included Rice, Lynn and Evans in the outfield, Yaz at first, Jerry Remy (acquired from California) at second, Rick Burleson at short, hard-hitting Butch Hobson at third and Fisk catching.

The Sox got off to a fast start and by mid-July were making a shambles of the race, leading the second-place Brewers by 10 and the fourth-place Yankees by 14½. Then the Sox began to tire, and Hobson developed a bad throwing arm (bone chips in the elbow) and began making errors at third at a record pace. Fisk was also getting weary and had some nagging injuries. But Zimmer refused to rest his players. In late July outfielder Paul Blair, a former Oriole now playing for the Yankees, commented that Zimmer should rest his team, especially with such a big lead, but Zimmer still didn't. Campbell was used too much and got

Above left: *Obtained in a trade with Cleveland, Dennis Eckersley won 20 games for the Sox in 1978.*

Above right: *Mike Torrez signed a big contract with the Red Sox prior to the 1978 season. Torrez won 16 games.*

a sore arm, and the team went from 62-28 on July 17 to 86-52 on September 6. Trailing by four games, the Yankees then came to Boston and produced the Boston Massacre of 1978, winning four straight by a 42-9 margin. New York moved into first.

The Sox came back, however, and on the last day of the season won their eighth in a row and ended up tied with the Yanks, who lost in Cleveland. A one-game playoff was slated for Fenway the next day, Monday, October 2. It was Torrez, who was 16-12, against the Yankees' young lefthanded flamethrower, Ron Guidry, who was 24-3.

Yaz homered, and the Sox led 2-0 after six. In the seventh the Yanks got one run and then singles from Chris Chambliss and Roy White. Then light-hitting shortstop Bucky Dent came up. He went to get some pine tar, and on-deck hitter Mickey Rivers looked at Dent's bat and saw a chip in it. "Get another," he advised.

Dent did, and he then hit a flyball down the leftfield line, just fair and just high enough to make the screen. The Yankees went up 4-2. In the eighth, off Stanley, who was the Sox relief ace with 18 wins, Reggie Jackson homered for a 5-2 lead. In the ninth the Red Sox scored two and had Burleson at first. Remy hit a shot into right field. Lou Piniella lost the ball in the sun but, kneeling down, put up his glove and caught the ball on the bounce. Burleson hesitated rounding second and didn't go to third. Remy had to hurry back to first. It should have been runners on second and third, with one out and Jim Rice and Carl Yastrzemski coming up. Instead it was first and second with one out. Rice hit a grounder that was a force play at second, and Burleson came to third. Yaz popped out against big reliever Rich Gossage. The Sox had blown a 10-game lead and lost the title.

Yankees' owner George Steinbrenner came into the Red Sox locker room after the 5-4 Yankee win, shook hands all around and said it was too bad one of the teams had to lose. "These are the two teams who should be playing for the World Series," he said. It was small consolation for the players and the fans. The Yanks went on to beat the Kansas City Royals for the AL flag and then beat the Dodgers again for the championship.

Zimmer never admitted to any mistakes in not resting players or in not getting an ailing Hobson out of the lineup. But the Sox did go on their eight-game winning streak at the end of the season with Hobson on the bench, and the fans never forgave Zimmer or Mike Torrez. Zim was the target of fan boos for the next two season, and Torrez was a marked man in Boston. The fans were so unforgiving that in 1983, five years later,

when the Sox were trying to contact Torrez to finalize a deal with the New York Mets, they had him paged at a Boston Bruins hockey game at Boston Garden. When the public address announcer asked for Mike Torrez to report to the press table, his announcement was greeted by a chorus of boos from the 14,000 at the hockey game.

Jim Rice did win the most valuable player award, for he had had an incredible season, batting .315, with 46 homers and 139 runs batted in, tops in the league in both. Eckersley won 20 games, but Tiant, in his final Boston season, was 13-8 and shocked Boston fans by signing with the Yankees as a free agent at the end of the season. Torrez won 16, although more had

been expected of him. Bill Lee won 10, and Lynn rebounded with a .298 average, 22 homers and 82 RBIs. Yaz had 145 hits and 17 homers.

Don Zimmer never could figure why fans were so down on him. "We won 97 in 1977, 99 in 1978, and 91 in 1979. That's pretty good baseball, I think" he said. But there were no championships, and he was wearing out his welcome.

In 1979 Lynn hit a league-leading .333 and had 39 homers and 122 RBIs. Rice batted .325, with 39 homers and 130 RBIs, but Eckersley fell to 17 wins, and Torrez had 16 again. Boston won 91 games and finished third, 11 behind Baltimore and four in back of Milwaukee. Highlights of the year were

Yaz' 3000th hit and his 400th homer. He was the first American Leaguer ever to do that and the 15th in major league history.

As 1980 approached so did an end to an era. All signs pointed to Lynn and Burleson and possibly Fisk going elsewhere, and Zimmer's job was on the line as well. In 1980 Boston dropped to fourth, 83-77, 20 in back of the Yankees, who won the AL East. Zimmer was let go with four games left, and Johnny Pesky finished.

Lynn hit .301, had 12 homers and 61 RBIs. Rice hit .294, with 24 HRs and 86 RBIs. Torrez was 9-16, and Eckersley 12-14. Lynn, Fisk and Burleson soon would be gone, and Mrs. Yawkey was about to assert herself for the Red Sox of the Eighties.

After his team blew a big lead and lost in the one-game playoff to the Yankees in 1978, manager Don Zimmer (above, number 34) became a target for unhappy fans.

9. Years of Turmoil

Below left: *Ralph Houk took over the Red Sox and led the club to a fifth-place finish in the strike-torn 1981 season. Houk skippered the troubled team through 1984.*

Below right: *In his first year with the Red Sox, third baseman Carney Lansford captured the 1981 American League batting title with a .336 average.*

After 4½ years – during which he won 715 games and had the fifth-best games-won record of all Red Sox managers and the sixth-best winning percentage (.575) of all Sox field bosses, Don Zimmer was out. He had won no championships and twice had had his team fade in the stretch. The Sox management saw that a time for healing was at hand.

What was needed was a man who could command respect, and even some affection, from the players and the fans. On October 27, 1980, Ralph Houk was lured out of retirement in Florida to become Boston's 35th manager. It was a challenge for the former skipper of the New York Yankees and Detroit Tigers, but he accepted it lightly. "I got tired of fishing everyday," he laughed when he took the job.

It wasn't long before he realized how serious his problems were going to be. On December 10 the Red Sox traded all-star shortstop Rick Burleson and third baseman Butch Hobson to California for Carney Lansford, Rick Miller and Mark Clear. It wasn't a bad deal for Boston, but it signaled that the 1975-era team was being seriously affected by the free agency situation that was buffeting all of baseball.

Burleson was unhappy with his negotiations with Boston and had hinted at free agency, and by the following January (1981) Fred Lynn was gone. It was not a good trade for Boston. The Sox had been working a deal with Los Angeles, which originally had coveted Lynn when he was in college. Boston was to get a starting pitcher and Mike Marshall, a slugging rookie who was slotted as the next Boston first baseman and was expected to tattoo

the leftfield wall. But Lynn and his agent wouldn't agree to a long-term contract, Los Angeles backed out and the Sox had to fall back to trading Lynn to the California Angels for Frank Tanana, Joe Rudi and Jim Dorsey. Only Tanana helped, and he only for two years. But since Lynn could be guaranteed for only a year it was the best deal available.

Houk had more or less expected these losses, although he had thought the team would get more for Lynn than it did. But the unexpected blow was the loss of Fisk. Haywood Sullivan, executive vice president and general manager, had neglected to mail a contract to Fisk by December 31. That meant the big catcher automatically became a free agent.

The Sox had tried in vain to negotiate with Fisk prior to that contractual gaffe, and as soon as he became a free agent Fisk checked around and accepted an offer from the Chicago White Sox. The Red Sox were devastated, and the fans were irate. Mrs Yawkey, now listed as president of the team, was unhappy too, and the close relationship she had had with Sullivan chilled a little, although they still needed each other to outvote Buddy LeRoux, whom they both disliked.

The team was in turmoil, but Houk proved adept at spreading oil on the troubled waters. He patiently got the players to believe in themselves and the team, and even calmed the fans, although the players' strike irritated the fans even more than did the trades. As it was, Boston ended the strike-torn year at 59-49, in fifth place, three games in back over-all, but four behind the first-half champion Yankees, and a game and a half behind second-half titlist Milwaukee. The Yanks then won the AL East title and took Oakland, the AL West champs, 3-0. But they lost the World Series to the Dodgers 4-2.

Best for the Sox that strike-shortened year were Bob Stanley and Mike Torrez, with 10 wins each. Tanana was 4-10. Mark Clear and Tom Burgmeier, a lefthanded reliever picked up in the free agent market, combined for 15 saves, nine by Clear. Lansford led the league at .336, and Jerry Remy hit .301, while Dwight Evans hit .296, with 22 homers and 71 RBIs, and Rice had 17 homers and 62 RBIs. Utility infielder Dave Stapleton hit .285, with 10 home runs.

Again Houk, known as "The Major" from his days as a U.S. Ranger during World War 2, kept the Sox clubhouse on an even keel in 1982, and while Boston helped make the season interesting, it was Milwaukee all the way, finishing at 95-67, one game ahead of the Orioles, and six up on third-place Boston. The Brewers would beat the Angels in the AL playoffs and then lose to St. Louis in the World Series.

Above left:
Outfielder Rick Miller at the plate. Miller, who was picked up along with Carney Lansford and pitcher Mark Clear from the California Angels before the 1981 season, had played for the Red Sox during the seventies.

Above right: *Second baseman Jerry Remy was a steady player for the Red Sox in his seven years with the team, 1978-1984.*

Boston's best that year was a bullpen featuring Clear, with 14 wins and 14 saves, and Stanley, with 12 wins and 14 saves. John Tudor, who had been a disappointing 4-3 in 1981, was 13-10. Eckersley was 13-13, and Torrez 9-9. He would soon be gone.

Lansford hit .301 that year, only his second, and his last as a Red Sox. Rice hit .309, with 24 homers and 97 RBIs, and Evans had another big year: .292, 32 homers and 98 RBIs. Yaz, heading toward the end of a career, hit .275, with 16 homers and 72 RBIs. A catcher named Rich Gedman from Worcester, Massachusetts, hit .249. A rookie also came up and surprised a lot of people: Wade Boggs had been the top hitter in the minors the previous year but had had a hard time staying with Boston. But once he got into the lineup on June 25, when Lansford was hurt, he stayed on and hit .349.

The off-season saw more changes. Lansford had gotten two substantial pay hikes in his two years at Boston, but he wanted an even bigger one and a long-term pact, and he was eligible for free agency at the end of 1983. So he was traded to Oakland for slugging outfielder Tony Armas.

Torrez, the target of boos the moment he had set foot on Fenway Park in 1978, went to the New York Mets for a minor league infielder in early 1983. The pitching staff now featured, in addition to Tudor and Eckersley, a lefthander who had won four in 1982, Bob Ojeda, and another lefty who was 3-7 but had disappointed over all, Bruce Hurst. Mark Clear had suddenly lost his control, and Stanley was now the entire bullpen.

Perhaps Houk's first year of disillusionment was 1983, not only because the team finished sixth, 78-84, 20 games back of Baltimore, but because of the infighting in the executive offices. Buddy LeRoux had been ever more critical of the way the team was being run. Mrs. Yawkey didn't like LeRoux, and she offered to buy him out. He retorted that he would buy her and Haywood out, and on June 6, 1983, matters came to a head.

This was to be a big night – Tony Conigliaro Night, to raise money to help pay the bills for the former Sox slugger who had suffered a stroke and was in a rehabilitation center. Teammates from the 1960s were coming to the game for the ceremonies. And that was the night that LeRoux moved. He got the support of a couple of limited partners, claimed he had control of the team and brought Dick O'Connell back as GM.

In the Fenway press room there were two different press conferences. The one headed by LeRoux announced that changes were about to come quickly. At the other con-

ference Haywood Sullivan was saying that nothing had changed and that he was still GM. It put a damper on Tony C Night and left fans, players and the Sox personnel bewildered.

Mrs. Yawkey took the matter to court. An injunction was issued, restoring the status quo, and eventually LeRoux lost in court, since the original agreement when the team was sold stipulated that it be run by a majority of the general partners, Mrs. Yawkey, LeRoux and Sullivan.

LeRoux's days were now numbered. Mrs. Yawkey was taking increasing control through her right-hand man, John Harrington, and Sullivan was being shoved aside, with ever more player decisions coming from Harrington. In February, 1984, James "Lou" Gorman was hired from the Mets to be general manager, taking over those duties from Sullivan, who now became chief executive officer and chief operating officer, titles with little power or responsibility. Like her husband before her, it was Jean Yawkey who was really running the Red Sox now.

In 1983 the Sox had a lefthanded pitching staff. Tudor won 13, Ojeda and Hurst 12 each and Eckersley fell to nine. (Over in New York Mike Torrez was 10-17.) The top hitters for the Sox in 1983 was Boggs, with a league-leading .361 and the first of six consecutive 200-hit seasons: he had 210 in 1983. Evans fell to .238, with 22 homers and 58 RBIs, and adopted a new hitting stance

the next season, one he would keep the next six years. Armas hit only .218 but had 36 homers and 107 RBIs, while Rice had another big year – .305, 39 homers and 126 RBIs, leading the league in homers and RBIs. Rich Gedman, with a .294 average, looked as though he might be headed for better things.

The year 1983 was also the end of another era. Yaz retired. He completed the 1983 season with a .266 average and with 101 hits and 10 homers. The future Hall of Famer ended his 23-year major league career (all with the Red Sox) with 3419 hits, 452 home runs, 1844 runs batted in, 3308 games and 1844 walks. He ranks second for all time in games played, third in times at bat, tied for 11th in runs scored (1816), seventh in hits, seventh in doubles, 18th in home runs and ninth in RBIs. There were two emotional days of goodbyes at the end of the 1983 season, with Yaz running around the park a couple of times to wave to, shake hands with and smile at the fans for the last time.

The following year, 1984, was Ralph Houk's final year. The turmoil, the tensions and the disappointments were taking their toll on the 65-year-old manager. The team finished in fourth place at 86-78, 18 behind the Detroit Tigers, who had opened the season by winning 25 of their first 30 games. The Tigers ultimately crushed the Kansas City Royals in the playoffs and the San Diego Padres in the World Series.

Boston again had mostly mediocrity on

Right: *Tom Seaver is joined at the mound by Red Sox manager John McNamara, catcher Rich Gedman, and second baseman Marty Barrett. Seaver won five games for Boston after coming over from the White Sox during the 1986 season.*

the mound, the top winners being Hurst, Ojeda, Dennis "Oil Can" Boyd (12 each) and rookie Al Nipper (11). In May Eckersley was traded to Chicago for first baseman Bill Buckner, who hit .278 for the Sox. Boggs again had more than 200 hits (203) and hit .325. Evans hit .295, with 32 homers and 104 RBIs. Armas had a big year, with a .268 average, a league-leading 43 homers and 128 RBIs. Rice hit .280, with 28 homers and 122 RBIs. Designated hitter Mike Easler, obtained in an off-season deal with Pittsburgh for Tudor, hit .313, with 27 homers and 91 RBIs. Gedman hit 24 homers and knocked in 72 runs.

At the end of 1984 Houk retired again. Haywood Sullivan's old teammate, John McNamara, was named manager in October of 1984. He had managed Oakland, San Diego, Cincinnati and California and had left the Angels at the end of the 1984 season.

He was considered a solid baseball man, dour, not popular with the media, but a pretty good skipper. Reportedly, Mrs. Yawkey and John Harrington had had some other candidates, including Joe Morgan, who had managed successfully at the Red Sox top farm club at Pawtucket from 1974 to 1982, but they deferred to Sullivan.

In 1985 the Sox finished dead even, 81-81, in fifth place in the East behind the Toronto Blue Jays, who finished 18 games ahead of the Sox. Boggs was the top hitter, with a .368 average and 240 hits. Buckner hit .299, with 16 homers and 110 RBIs. Evans hit .263, with 29 homers and 73 RBIs; Gedman had .295, 18 homers and 80 RBIs; Rice was at .291, with 27 homers and 103 RBIs; and Armas fell off to 23 homers and 64 RBIs. Boyd led in pitching, with 15 wins, Hurst had 11 and a kid named Roger Clemens was 7-5 but had had shoulder surgery in August. Clemens was Boston's top draft choice in 1983, and it was hoped he could still have a big career. All in all, it was not an auspicious start for John McNamara, but both better and worse were to come.

Above: *Red Sox great Carl Yastrzemski acknowledges the cheers at Fenway after belting a three-run homer in midseason, 1983. Yastrzemski retired later that year. Yaz was inducted into the Hall of Fame in 1989.*

Left: *Al Nipper won 11 games for the Red Sox as a rookie in 1984. Nipper was shipped to the Cubs following the 1987 season.*

10. The Improbable Year

Right: Dennis "Oil Can" Boyd winds up for a pitch. Boyd posted a 16-10 record in the pennant-winning season of 1986. The fiery pitcher had problems with injuries in his years with the Red Sox.

There was no reason for Red Sox fans to get particularly worked up about the 1986 season. No phenoms like Lynn or Rice were coming up from the farm system, and the team had a lot of question marks, including Roger Clemens, with his shoulder surgery of the previous August.

Even when the Sox traded designated hitters with the Yankees, exchanging Mike Easler for Don Baylor, there wasn't much fan reaction. Both, after all, were aging veterans, and hadn't Yankees' owner George Steinbrenner written Baylor off by saying he wouldn't be visible by August? Most New England sports fans were either talking about the New England Patriots' Super Bowl season or wondering whether the Boston Celtics could repeat as National Basketball Association champions. The smart baseball money was betting on the Yankees or the Blue Jays in the AL East.

But the Sox got off to a reasonable start, and Clemens reassured everyone by winning his first three starts. It wasn't until April 29 that it suddenly dawned on Sox fans that maybe 1986 was going to be something special. On that night Clemens shut down the Seattle Mariners at Fenway Park before a modest crowd of 13,414. Roger struck out 20 Mariners, setting a single-game major league record, and Boston rallied in the eighth to give Clemens a 3-1 win and national recognition for the strikeout record. The win hiked the Sox' record to 11-8 and left them 2½ out of first. Still, it was early in the season and no time to get worked up about the prospects.

On May 11 "Oil Can" Boyd stopped the Oakland A's 6-5, and Boston moved into first place by a game. The Sox hiked it to two the next day, then dropped out two days later, trailing by a half game, and then went back into first for good on May 17, when Boyd beat the Texas Rangers 8-2.

The lead was tenuous for two weeks, never more than 2½ games into June, but then it went to 5 when Clemens won his 10th straight game, 3-0, over Milwaukee on June 6. They increased it to 6½ by winning three from the Yankees in New York, but injuries to the pitching staff were beginning to take their toll.

Nipper had suffered a deep cut in the muscle under his right knee when he was run into at home plate by the Rangers' Larry Parrish. Nipper tagged Parrish out but was out of action from May 18 until June 25. Bruce Hurst had pulled a groin muscle May 31 in Minnesota and didn't return until July 18.

McNamara juggled the staff. He used Clemens and Boyd, and then tried Rob Woodward and Jeff Sellers, rookies up from Pawtucket. He also tried Mike Brown, who had been a rising star in 1983, his rookie year, but was stymied by injuries that kept him going between Boston and Pawtucket. The two relievers obtained from the New York Mets in a trade for Bob Ojeda were not helping: Wes Gardner had to have shoulder surgery, and Calvin Schiraldi had started at Pawtucket and wouldn't be recalled until late July.

The bullpen was in the hands of Steve Crawford and Bob Stanley, who had had a terrible 1985 season after he had to have hand surgery to remove a growth. The fans were vicious to Stanley, who got booed so badly one day that he stood in the locker room after the game and said, "My only prayer is that I am on the mound the day we clinch the pennant, and I can look at all those fans and smile and salute them." Joe Sambito, a lefthander who had been a standout for Houston for years, was signed as a free agent and helped out the bullpen a lot, especially early in the season.

With that makeshift pitching staff, the Sox came home after sweeping New York and lost two of three to Baltimore. Then they lost the first two of a series with the Yankees. The lead was now down to 4, and a

Yankee sweep might have a major psychological effect on the Sox. Instead they got a huge boost.

Nipper, who had been recovering much faster than the doctors expected, said he was ready. He was reactivated on June 25 and beat the Yankees 5-4 in a gutsy performance, with his right knee still not at full strength. It touched off a six-game winning streak that pushed Boston to eight up in the standings.

Clemens won his first 14 games, finally

Top: *Bob Stanley had 16 saves coming out of the bullpen in 1986. Unfortunately, he will always be remembered by Red Sox fans for the wild pitch that allowed the Mets to tie, then win, game six of the World Series.*

Below: *Designated hitter Don Baylor belts a long ball. Baylor's presence in the Red Sox lineup helped the club capture the American League flag in 1986. Baylor smacked 31 homers and drove in 94 runs.*

Right: *Southpaw Bruce Hurst provided the Red Sox with a solid effort during the stretch drive in 1986. Hurst, who was 13-8 overall, went 5-0 in the month of September.*

Right: *Roger Clemens gets ready to unleash a pitch at Fenway in the AL championship series. The Rocket put together an explosive 1986 season, beginning with his record-setting 20-strikeout game in April; he went on to win 24 games. The hard-throwing pitcher was awarded Cy Young and Most Valuable Player honors.*

ting in the clutch and providing leadership in the clubhouse. Buckner was playing with bad ankles but was hitting and fielding well, while Jim Rice was bouncing back handsomely from two so-so seasons. Rich Gedman was an All-Star catcher. If there was any problem, it was at shortstop, where highly-touted rookie Rey Quinones was playing and hitting .233.

General Manager Lou Gorman moved quickly to beef up the team for the pennant drive. He traded Quinones to Seattle for switch-hitting shortstop Spike Owen and centerfielder Dave Henderson. Henderson provided backup in center for Tony Armas, who was hitting only .264, with 11 homers and 58 RBIs. Tony was having trouble getting around on the ball and slowed down in center as well, and Henderson platooned with him during the last month or so of the season. Owen took over at short and, while not spectacular, did help solidify the infield.

Hurst came back and lost his first two starts after being reactivated in July. He went 3-2 in August and 5-0 in September, with a 1.07 ERA. Schiraldi didn't allow a run in his 11 straight relief outings. The Sox went from 56-32 at the All-Star break to 76-54 at the end of August but saw their lead fall to 3½. Then they went on an 11-game winning streak, and the race was in doubt no longer. The team finally clinched the division title when Boyd beat Toronto 12-3 on September 28.

This had been a real surprise. A group of veterans had put it together with a couple of young pitchers who had been question marks at the start of the season. Gorman had made some shrewd moves, including acquiring Henderson and Owen and getting veteran star Tom Seaver from the Chicago White Sox for highly touted utility player Steve Lyons. Seaver came aboard on July 1 and won his opener 9-7 over Toronto; over-all he was only 5-7 with Boston, but he provided great leadership during the pressure days. Unfortunately, he pulled a muscle at the end of the season and could not play in either the playoffs or the World Series, and he would be gone after the season, his great career ended.

In the playoffs the California Angels were the opposition. They had won the West with a 92-70 mark, five ahead of second-place Texas. Boston was 95-66, 5½ up on the second-place Yankees. Mike Witt beat Clemens in the first game of the series, 8-1, at Fenway Park. Brian Downing had two two-run singles off Clemens. Witt gave up only five hits.

Game 2, also at Fenway, went to Hurst, who gave up 11 hits but only two runs, and Boston beat Kirk McCaskill 9-2. Boston scored three unearned runs in the seventh

losing to Oakland 5-4. He went 15-2 to the All-Star break, then went out to pitch three scoreless innings for the American League and was the winning pitcher and the game's most valuable player. When the All-Star game ended Hurst came off the disabled list, and the Sox were ready for the run for the roses.

Don Baylor was having a great year, hit-

Left: *Tom Seaver was a clubhouse leader for Boston in 1986, but was unable to perform in the post-season.*

Below: *Dave Henderson allows a Bobby Grich drive to go off his glove for a homer in the sixth inning of the fifth game of the 1986 ALCS against California. Henderson would make up for it at the plate, his sacrifice fly scoring the winning run.*

Red Sox second baseman Marty Barrett was the ALCS MVP with 11 hits. He enjoyed a fine World Series as well, collecting 13 hits in 30 trips to the plate.

to boost a 3-2 lead. Jim Rice and Wally Joyner of the Angels homered.

The series then moved to Anaheim, California, where veteran lefthander John Candelaria shut down the Sox, California winning 5-3, with Oil Can Boyd giving up two-out homers in the seventh to Dick Schofield and Gary Pettis, as the Angels snapped a 1-1 tie. Rich Gedman had three hits and two runs batted in.

Games 4 and 5 were emotional roller coasters. On Saturday night Clemens held the Angels scoreless through eight innings and Boston had chipped away for a run in the sixth and two in the eighth off Don Sutton. But by the ninth Clemens was tiring, and McNamara ran into the first of the criticism of his managing when he left Roger in. By the time he got Schiraldi in, the Angels had scored twice, and then, with two out, the rookie hit Brian Downing with a 1-2 pitch to force in the tying run. Bobby Grich singled in the winning run in the 11th, and the Sox were down 3-1 in the series and shaken.

It appeared that the series was all over on Sunday afternoon when Witt went to the mound against Hurst. Gedman hit a two-run homer in the second to give the Sox the lead. Bob Boone homered in the third to cut it to 2-1, and in the sixth Grich hit a long drive to center. Henderson, having replaced a slowed-down Armas, raced to the wall, leaped up and had the ball in his glove; but when the glove hit the top of the fence the ball popped out for a two-run home run. The Angels added two in the seventh off Hurst and Stanley, and it was

5-2 going into the ninth. The 64,233 California fans were rocking and singing and cheering and standing: World Series here we come!

But wait a minute! In the ninth Buckner led off with a single, and after one out Baylor, who had hit 31 homers during the season, homered to left, and it was 5-4. Evans popped out, and then manager Gene Mauch started making moves. He brought in lefthander Gary Lucas to pitch to lefthander Gedman. Lucas hit Gedman with a pitch. Out went Lucas and in came flame-throwing reliever Donnie Moore, who had been having a tough year. He faced Henderson, got to 2-2 on him, and then Henderson smashed a home run to left, and Boston led 6-5.

And still it was not over. In the last of the ninth the Angels tied the game and had the bases loaded and one out, but Steve Crawford worked out of the jam. The game went into extra innings. In the 11th Henderson hit a sacrifice fly to win it for Boston 7-6, and he became an instant cult hero in New England and throughout the nation.

The stunned Angels were badly shaken. Back in Boston the Sox scored five in the third off McCaskill, and Boyd cruised to a 10-4 win. The series was now tied at 3. In Game 7 Clemens pitched seven scoreless innings, and this time McNamara showed that he had learned his lesson and brought in Schiraldi. Boston cruised to victory, 8-1, with Jim Rice hitting a three-run homer. Marty Barrett was named the series MVP, with 11 hits in 30 at bats for a .367 average. Now it was on to New York and the Mets in the World Series.

The Red Sox were on a roll, and the Mets had to bear the brunt of it. The Series opened Saturday night in chilly Shea Stadium, and Bruce Hurst outdueled Ron Darling as Boston won 1-0. Hurst gave up four hits in eight innings, and Schiraldi got the Mets in the ninth. Darling deserved a better fate. The only run off him came in the seventh when he walked Rice. Rice then went to second on a wild pitch and scored when Gedman's grounder went through the legs of second baseman Tim Teufel. Boston had only five hits.

Game 2 on Sunday had Clemens against Dwight Gooden, and the Sox again prevailed, but neither Roger nor Dwight were around at the end when Boston won 9-3. The Sox scored three in the third, and the Mets got two back in the last of the third. Henderson hit a solo homer in the fourth and Evans hit a two-run homer in the fifth. Overall Boston had 18 hits, and Crawford was the winning pitcher, coming in in the fifth. Stanley pitched the last three.

Boyd was on the mound in Game 3, and

he was a sight for sore Met eyes. They clubbed him at Fenway for four in the first and sailed to a 7-1 win behind Bob Ojeda's five-hit pitching. Len Dykstra, the Mets' center fielder, led off the game with a homer, and the Mets never trailed. They had 13 hits to Boston's five.

Game 4 could have seen a return of Hurst, but McNamara went with Al Nipper. He pitched until the fourth, when New York scored three times and went on to a 6-2 win in which Gary Carter hit two homers. Darling was the winner. Boston had seven hits, three by Gedman and two by Barrett.

McNamara looked good when Hurst came back in Game 5 and stopped New York 4-2, giving up 10 hits in a route-going performance. Gooden was the loser, with Boston scoring one each in the second and third, and two in the fifth, while the Mets got one each in the eighth and ninth, the latter being Tim Teufel's home run.

Game 6 will go into the annals of the World Series as one of the most incredible games ever. It was Clemens against Ojeda at Shea. The Sox scored single runs in the first and second, and the Mets tied with two in the fifth. Clemens developed a blister in the seventh and left the game, Schiraldi coming on. Boston scored in the seventh, and the Mets got it back in the eighth.

In the 10th Henderson hit a lead-off homer, and the Sox added another run for a 5-3 lead. Schiraldi got the first two batters in the last of the 10th, but Gary Carter kept the Mets' hopes alive with a two-strike single. Kevin Mitchell then pinch hit for the pitcher and singled. Stanley was warming up in the bullpen, but McNamara stuck with Schiraldi. Ray Knight singled, and the Mets had cut the lead to 5-4. Out went Schiraldi and in came Stanley. He threw an inside pitch, and Gedman couldn't hold it. It was ruled a wild pitch, and Mitchell came in with the tying run.

And then, in a play played over and over on television, Mookie Wilson hit a grounder down the firstbase line. Buckner was playing deep, and when he tried to field the ball it went through his legs. Knight scored, and the Sox had lost 6-5.

Technically, the Sox still had a chance, but neither they nor anyone else really believed it. It rained on Sunday, but all that did was delay the inevitable. Just as Game 5 of the AL playoffs had doomed the Angels, Game 6 had done the same for the Sox.

McNamara reduced Boyd to tears by telling him that he would not pitch Monday because McNamara was going back to Hurst. Bruce went six innings, giving up four hits and three runs. Once again McNamara went to Schiraldi, who was probably the most shellshocked of the Sox pitchers after Game 6. The Mets feasted on him for three runs in a third of an inning, and the New Yorkers won 8-5, to win the Series. It was an improbable end to an improbable season. It also was the beginning of the end for John McNamara as Red Sox manager.

Red Sox catcher Rich Gedman attempts to tag out the Mets' Gary Carter during the 1986 World Series. Carter smacked two homers and drove in nine runs for the New Yorkers.

11. Wait Till Next Year!

In 1986 Roger Clemens won 25, lost 4, struck out 238 and was named the AL's most valuable player and the Cy Young Award winner. Six months later the fans were booing him at Fenway Park. John McNamara was named AL manager of the year, yet he was booed when he stepped on the field on opening day of 1987.

They also booed Bob Stanley and Calvin Schiraldi. They would doubtless have booed Rich Gedman for not catching the ball in the 10th inning of Game 6, but he wasn't there on opening day. He had opted for free agency, not signing with anyone and having to wait until May 1 to rejoin the Sox.

The fans cheered Dave Henderson and Don Baylor, but they hooted Bill Buckner. The boos that had greeted Jim Rice for two so-so years in 1984 and 1985 became cheers for his .324, 200-hit, 20-homer, 110-RBI season. They would turn to jeers later as he suffered through a .277, 13-homer, 62-RBI 1987. Rice had been number three on the MVP voting in 1986. What a difference a year makes.

Clemens earned about $400,000 in 1986, what with incentives and all. But he wanted more than a million dollars in 1987

and walked out of training camp and continued to hold out until just a day or two before the season began. He signed for about $1 million, but now he was not in shape for the season and went 4-6 before straightening out and winning 20 and losing 9, with 256 strikeouts. He was named Cy Young Award winner again, but the Sox stumbled home at 78-84, 20 games in back of the Tigers, who caught Toronto on the next to last day of the season.

Mrs. Yawkey and Harrington were in favor of firing McNamara then, but they were talked out of it by Sullivan and Gorman, who cited the various problems McNamara had had, including Hurst coming down with mononucleosis and not being able to win in the latter part of the season. Oil Can Boyd missed most of the season and had shoulder surgery in August. The other veterans who had produced in 1986 didn't do so in 1987. Before the year was over Buckner, Baylor and Henderson would be gone.

Evans had a big year, batting .305, with 34 homers and 123 RBIs. And there were newcomers who had been forced onto McNamara, who preferred veterans. But he

After a strong 1986 season in which he finished third in the MVP voting, left fielder Jim Rice struggled through a mediocre year in 1987. Rice hit just 13 homers and drove in just 62 runs.

Left: *The 1987 season proved to be the final one in Boston for reliever Calvin Schiraldi. Schiraldi and Al Nipper were traded to the Chicago Cubs for bullpen ace Lee Smith.*

Far left: *Right fielder Dewey Evans runs the basepaths. In his sixteenth season, Dwight Evans clouted 34 home runs and drove in 123 runs.*

was playing Ellis Burks in center, and he hit .272, with 20 homers and 27 stolen bases. There was also leftfielder-DH Mike Greenwell, who hit .328, with 19 homers and 89 RBIs. And there was big Sam Horn at DH, belting 14 homers in 46 games.

Gedman had finally signed and had had a miserable season, being injured early, coming back and then being out for the rest of the year with torn ligaments in his thumb. He hit .205. Everything had gone wrong in 1987, but the newcomers made 1988 look hopeful.

One thing was certain for the Red Sox management after 1987: they had to find a relief pitcher – a top stopper. But even General Manager Lou Gorman was surprised that he could lay his hands on Lee Smith, the huge fireballing reliever from the Chicago Cubs. The 6-foot, 6-inch, 240-pounder had saved 36 games in 1987 for the lowly Cubs and had saved 30 or more four years in a row, for a total of 163 in five seasons.

He had saved more than twice as many games as had the entire Red Sox staff in 1987, when Boston had 16 saves for the season. Obviously the Sox wanted him, but they didn't think he was available. In Chicago, with a new general manager and old Red Sox friend Don Zimmer as manager, they knew they needed pitching. They also felt that Smith, who was 30, might have seen his best days. So the Sox sent the 1986 World Series hero and goat, Calvin Schiraldi, and pitcher Al Nipper to the Cubs for Smith.

The trade fired the imaginations of New England fans, and talk of the pennant was everywhere and carried on into spring training. The Sox were by now a much changed team. Buckner was gone, traded to California and later to end up in Kansas City. Dave Henderson had been traded to San Francisco; he later was released and went to Oakland, where he would have a fantastic season in Oakland's pennant drive. Don Baylor had left the Sox in time to join Minnesota and be in the 1987 World Series; then he signed with the A's and would be in the 1988 World Series. Three years, three different teams and three World Series for Baylor.

The 1988 Sox had none of the contract disputes that had created problems in 1987. And there was a lot of young talent looking very good. The only dispute was whether Mike Greenwell or Jim Rice would play left. Most thought it should be Greenwell. Rice, and later Manager John McNamara, favored Rice, and that would be part of Johnny Mac's downfall. In spring training the team looked so good it was scary, and many observers were saying the Sox were the team to beat in 1988.

But there were some problems. McNamara had always liked veterans. He didn't care how well Jody Reed played in spring training; Spike Owen was to be his shortstop. And he didn't particularly care for young Todd Benzinger, and insisted on Dwight Evans at first, although Evans was having defensive problems there.

Still, things looked good, and advance ticket sales were big. Boston started off all right, going 14-6 in the first month. But there were indications of problems waiting to surface. They surfaced in May, when the Sox went 11-16. Jim Rice was having serious hitting problems and went from

Above: *Mike Greenwell found himself in a battle for the left field job with veteran Jim Rice during the 1988 season. The youngster proved his worth with 22 homers and 119 RBI.*

Below: *Todd Benzinger puts the tag on Yankee Rickey Henderson. Benzinger was a rookie first baseman in 1987, and was traded to the Cincinnati Reds prior to the 1989 campaign.*

leftfielder to designated hitter and even, for a short spell, to the bench. He could no longer hit the fastball. Evans was having problems at first, and it affected his hitting. Owen was at short, but he was not hitting well, and even Smith was having some problems; he began by giving up a winning home run to Detroit's Alan Trammell on the opening day at Fenway Park. Rumors were rife that McNamara was on the spot.

The more the rumors were repeated, the more McNamara used his veterans, apparently afraid to trust his future to rookies. In June Boston went 14-12 but lost Jeff Sellers when he was hit by a line drive in Cleveland and broke his hand. Wes Gardner was taken from the bullpen to become a starter. But the fans and the Mrs. Yawkey were losing patience.

At All-Star break the Sox were 43-42,

nine in back of the Tigers in the AL East. It was then that Mrs. Yawkey decided. Despite the protestations of both Haywood Sullivan and Lou Gorman, she decided that McNamara had to go. She was now the power, having bought out general partner Buddy LeRoux the previous winter. And since the firing came so suddenly, the Sox took what appeared to be a stopgap measure: they named third-base coach Joe Morgan to be interim manager.

The 58-year-old Morgan, a native of nearby Walpole, had been in baseball for 36 years, ever since he had signed with the Boston Braves after he came out of Boston College. He had spent 15 years in the minor leagues as an infielder, had had a couple of brief stints in the majors with Milwaukee, Kansas City, Philadelphia, Cleveland and St. Louis and had begun managing in the Pittsburgh organization in 1966. He had joined the Red Sox in 1974, had managed at Pawtucket from 1974 to 1982, was International League manager of the year in 1977 and became a Sox scout in 1983. In 1985 he became a Sox coach. He had applied for the Sox managing job in 1981, when Ralph Houk was hired, and again in 1985, when McNamara was chosen. Now he had it on an interim basis. That basis didn't last long.

Joe's first day as manager was rained out, but on July 15 Roger Clemens outpitched Kansas City's Saberhagen at Fenway Park 3-1. The Red Sox would then win 12 in a row. They would go from 9 games back to a game and a half out in those 12 days, as both the Tigers and Yankees fell on hard times. Fans were beginning to think that maybe it could happen again.

It was called "Morgan's Miracle," and, indeed, Joe had a lot to do with it. The team had been uptight before Joe took over. There was serious dissension between the veterans favored by and backing McNamara and the young players. In addition, there was considerable discontent over the Wade Boggs palimony case. In May a California woman had sued Wade Boggs, claiming she was his on-the-road wife, joining him on extended Red Sox road trips, and that he had promised to take care of her financially.

When she and Wade broke up in early 1988 she decided to sue, and she named others on the Red Sox who might be subpoenaed to testify to her relationship with Wade. Wade Boggs eventually apologized to the team for the problem; he admitted that he and Margo had been together on road trips, but he said that it was all over and that he had promised her nothing. This didn't seem to affect Boggs, who was hitting as well as ever, but it did cause tension on

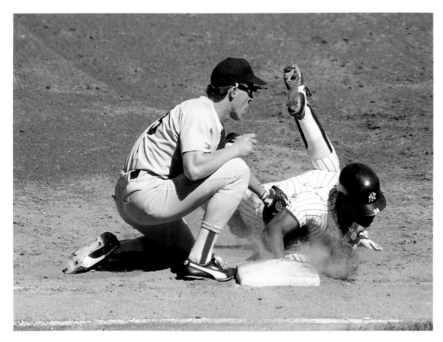

the team, including a near fight in Cleveland between pro- and anti-Boggs players.

John McNamara hadn't really known how to handle this situation and had tried to distance himself from it. But it wouldn't go away, and it hurt the team and eventually helped bring John McNamara down. Morgan couldn't solve the situation either, but he created such a relaxed atmosphere in the clubhouse and dugout that at least the controversy became less of an issue.

But Morgan could assert his authority when necessary. One night he put in a pinch hitter for Jim Rice. Rice fumed, yelled at Morgan and grabbed him. Morgan's reaction was instantaneous. Rice was suspended and fined; later he apologized. Morgan was indeed in charge. And how could anyone argue with a man whose team set an American League record with 25 consecutive home victories and who went from 43-42 on July 14 to 66-50 (23-8) in 30 days?

The Sox hired Joe as permanent manager for two years. He was the talk of all baseball, as were the Red Sox, who now were 2½ games out and looking very good.

Several changes had been made in the team. Evans was moved back to right field where he had been a Golden Glove fielder for a decade. Benzinger and Lance Parish, picked up from Texas, were assigned to first. Owen sat down, and Jody Reed became a standout at short. Even injuries like the shoulder problems of Dennis Boyd and the viral infection of Bruce Hurst and Sellers, again out of action with bone chips in his ankle, couldn't stop the team.

The Sox picked up Mike Boddicker from Baltimore in a late July trade for Brady Anderson, who had been a phenom in spring training but had not played well when the season started, and a minor league pitcher. Boddicker, the ace of the Baltimore staff, went 7-3 in Boston and gave the team a solid 1-2-3 pitching punch (with Roger Clemens and Bruce Hurst). Gardner, too, was pitching well, and Lee Smith was outstanding out of the bullpen.

The Sox had the staggers after that big start under Morgan, but the Tigers and Yankees, Toronto and Milwaukee had worse problems. Boston went 23-23 in the final month and a half, took over first place on September 5 and never left. They had two big series with the Yankees. The first brought the Yanks into Boston for a four-game set, with the Yanks 4½ back. Inevitably, there were some haunting memories of the Boston Massacre of 1978, when the Yankees came to Boston four out and took all four games en route to a playoff for the pennant. New York won the opener this time, but before talk of the Massacre could go any further Boston won the next three.

Joe Morgan was named interim manager at the All-Star break in 1988. Morgan, who had been the third base coach, took a team which was nine games out of first and helped it to a divisional crown.

Then, after a bad road trip to Toronto, the Sox came into Yankee Stadium, up by four, and won two of three to just about clinch the AL East flag. Unfortunately, the hitting slump the team had been in for a while reasserted itself, and the Sox lost three to Toronto at Boston, but then they crushed Cleveland 12-0 on September 29 to clinch a tie for first. The Yanks and Milwaukee lost the next day, and the division title was Boston's. It wasn't fancy, 89-73, a game ahead of Detroit, two up on Toronto and Milwaukee and 3½ ahead of New York, but it was a championship.

Oakland, meanwhile, had taken the lead in May and never lost it, winning 104 games and taking the AL West by 13 over Minnesota. The playoffs would open in Boston, and Sox fans were worried about the Boston offense. The Red Sox led the league in hitting, at .283, in runs scored, with 813, and in runs batted in, with 760. But the Sox had hit under .200 during the last week of the season.

The Sox lost the first game of the playoffs 2-1, as Dave Stewart and two Oakland relievers outpitched Bruce Hurst, who was Boston's top pitcher at 18-6. Jose Canseco, the top home run hitter in the majors, with 42, and RBIs, with 126, homered for one run, but after Boston tied in the seventh on a sacrifice fly by Boggs the A's won it on a single by Dave Henderson.

It was a worrisome game, since the Red Sox had had three major opportunities to blow it open. Boggs had struck out with the bases loaded in the second. He had driven in

Above: *Shortstop Jody Reed turned in a solid 1988 season, batting .293 in 109 games.*

Right: *Roger Clemens winds up. Clemens pitched well in 1988 despite a back injury, going 18-12 with a league-leading 14 complete games.*

one run – but left two stranded – in the seventh. And then in the ninth, with the tying run on second and the winning run at first, he had struck out again. In all, he had left seven of the eight runners he had on base stranded. A disappointment from the man who led the majors with a .366 average and 214 hits.

Game 2 was to rely on Clemens, who had finished the year at 18-12 after suffering a back injury while laying some carpet at his home during the season. It still affected his pitching, but he threw six solid shutout innings in Game 2. The Sox could do little against Storm Davis until the last of the sixth, when an error by Henderson in center and a single by Ellis Burks gave Boston a 2-0 lead. But in the top of the seventh Henderson singled and Canseco homered. Then a single, a balk and a single by Mark McGwire gave Oakland a 3-2 lead. Boston tied in the last of the seventh on a Rich Gedman homer. Lee Smith pitched out of a jam in the eighth but gave up a run in the ninth on three singles, the last by rookie short-stop Walt Weiss. Dennis Eckersley came in as he had the night before and got the Sox out, his 46th and 47th saves of the season.

In Oakland for Game 3 the Sox broke out of the slump against Bob Welch, scoring five runs in the first two innings, with Mike

Left: *Mike Boddicker went 7-3 after coming over from the Orioles during the 1988 season. Boddicker was a major factor in Boston's drive to the top of the American League Eastern Division.*

Greenwell, who had hit .325, with 22 homers and 119 runs batted in, doubling in two runs and homering for another. But Mike Boddicker, who hadn't allowed a home run in his last seven outings, was racked by the A's, including a two-run homer by Ron Hassey and a solo shot by Mark McGwire, and Boston lost 10-6.

Game 4 saw the Sox return to their hitting problems as Stewart and the A's won, 4-1. The Sox lost their big chance in the first when Dwight Evans struck out with the bases loaded. Hurst was the loser. Eckersley got the save, his fourth in four games, and he was named the most valuable player of the playoffs. The Red Sox had been swept out of the league championship.

Oakland thus joined the Dodgers of Los Angeles in an all-California World Series, which, surprisingly enough, the Dodgers won, taking the Series in five games.

Boston, meanwhile, went home. Morgan said graciously that the better team had won the playoffs but that his team would make a few moves to shore up a couple of areas and would be back next year ready to defend. Uncertain were the fates of Rice and Bob Stanley, who had a so-so year in relief, and Owen, who wanted to be traded. Lee Smith had 29 saves, and appeared ready for another big year in 1989. Clemens expected to be healed and hale.

Left: *Big reliever Lee Smith proved his worth in 1988, coming out of the bullpen to post 29 saves. Smith appeared in 64 games in his first season with the Red Sox.*

The 1989 season started off with high hopes and expectations for the Boston Red Sox. The defending American League East champions apparently had been strengthened by two off-season deals, one with Cincinnati bringing first baseman Nick Esasky and left-handed reliever Rob Murphy, and the other with Montreal which gave Boston right-handed pitcher John Dopson and utility infielder Luis Rivera. Additionally, Jim Rice and Bob Stanley, disappointments in 1988, apparently were healthy and poised for big comebacks, and Dennis "Oil Can" Boyd had recovered from the blood clot in his shoulder and was being counted on for a 15-win season.

The lone dark cloud was the Wade Boggs story, with Boggs' ex-girlfriend Margo Adams suing him for millions on her claim that their on-the-road affair of four years had cost her lost income. Adams also threatened to drag Boggs' teammates into the palimony case. Rumors of Boggs being traded abounded during spring training and even after. He insisted he wanted to stay, and none of the deals materialized. Adams lost much of her case when a judge ruled against her getting millions in damages. Eventually the Adams issue, including a tell-all, two-part article in *Penthouse*, faded, but Boston's other problems mounted.

Injuries hit the team hard, including a recurrence of the blood clot problem that kept Boyd sidelined until the last month of the season. Roger Clemens, the workhorse of

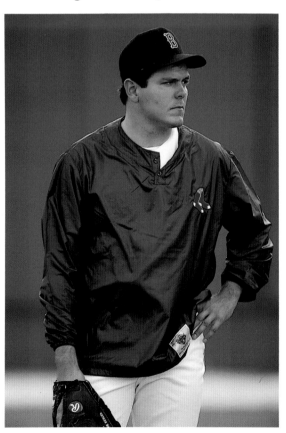

Left-handed relief pitcher Rob Murphy, acquired by the Sox from the Reds in the '89 off-season, quickly became a bullpen ace.

the staff, had a muscle tear that had him pitching in pain much of the year, and he ended with 17 wins rather than the 20 or more expected in March. Jim Rice was sidelined with bone chips in the elbow that required surgery, and injuries set down center fielder Ellis Burks, left fielder Mike Greenwell, second baseman Marty Barrett, and designated hitters Sam Horn and Carlos Quintana. Manager Joe Morgan could not field his regular starting lineup for nearly two-thirds of the season.

The Sox were under .500 most of the year, and it took a streak of winning 10 of the last 12 games to get them to a final record of 83-79. They closed to within a game of first in August, but blew a 6-0 lead against Baltimore in a key game, lost the game, lost the chance to move into first, and then went on a disastrous trip to the West Coast, winning the first game at Oakland, and then losing eight in a row to just about drop out of contention. Toronto eventually held off Baltimore to win the AL East crown, and Boston finished six back in third place.

Other low points included the Sox stranding more than 1000 baserunners during the season, and the ends of the Red Sox careers of Jim Rice and Bob Stanley. Both were in the final year of their multi-million dollar contracts, and were told that the Sox would not be exercising the option of signing them again. A bitter Rice said he was not through, criticized Red Sox management, and said he would try to sign with another team. He declined a special day at the end of the season to honor him. Stanley, saying he could tell it was time to end his career, decided to retire, and was honored on the final day of the season.

Although the Sox struggled for much of the season, there were some highlights. Nick Esasky had a big year with 30 home runs and 108 runs batted in. Rob Murphy became the ace of the bullpen. John Dopson won 12 games, and after a slow start Mike Boddicker went on a tear and ended with a 15-11 record. Burks, although injured twice in the season, batted .303. Greenwell had a sharp drop off in home runs, from 22 in 1988 to 14 in 1989, and dipped from a batting average of .325 in 1988 to .308 in 1989. Wade Boggs, despite struggling all season, did achieve his seventh consecutive 200-hit season, the most since Ty Cobb did it nine times for the Detroit Tigers. Boggs ended hitting .330, but after winning four consecutive AL batting crowns, he had to settle for third place behind new hitting champ Kirby Puckett, and Carney Lansford.

High points of the season included Wade Boggs' reaching the 200-hit and 100-walk mark for the fourth consecutive season, breaking the major league record held by

Nick Esasky at the plate in spring training, after coming to the Red Sox in the same deal that brought Rob Murphy. The popular first baseman was an asset at the plate, belting 30 home runs and knocking in 108 runs in 1989.

Hall of Famer Lou Gehrig. Dwight Evans hit 20 home runs for a ninth consecutive season and for the eleventh time in the last 12 years. And, to bring back the glories of Red Sox past, Carl Yastrzemski was inducted into the Baseball Hall of Fame in July, and his uniform number was retired in a touching ceremony at Fenway later in the summer.

There were some encouraging signs at the end of the season as well. Rookie catcher John Marzano, who spent the season in Pawtucket, batted over .400 for Boston in the final month, while Boyd finally

came back and pitched well in three outings in September.

The 1989 season mirrored three other post-championship seasons for the team. In 1967 the Red Sox won the pennant, and in 1968 they finished fourth. In 1975 they won the pennant and in 1976 they came in third, and 1986 was a pennant year and 1987 saw the team finish fifth.

But the team did set a record with more than two and a half million fans filling Fenway for the season, proving that they are the team of eternal hope, and that their rooters, in the end, are not fair-weather fans.

12. The Curse of the Bambino

Four years after the Red Sox meltdown in the 1986 World Series, *Boston Globe* columnist Dan Shaughnessy wrote a book called *The Curse of the Bambino*. Every BoSox heartbreak, Shaughnessy said (only a bit tongue in cheek), flowed like water downhill from the 1920 sale of Babe Ruth to the Yankees. Certainly the events of 1990–2003 did little to dispel The Curse mythology.

In 1990, Boston started the new decade on a positive note, winning the American League East title for the third time in five years. Manager Joe Morgan's team stayed close all season long, never dropping below third place and never more than four games out of first. The team batted .272, and the pitching staff, headed by Roger Clemens, did their job. Roger went 21-6, and had a league best ERA of 1.93. The Sox had decided that they could not have two closers so they traded Lee Smith to the Cardinals for outfielder Tom Brunansky and picked up free agent Jeff Reardon (from Dalton in the Berkshires of Massachusetts). Reardon proved a good fit—he appeared in 47 games and had 21 saves.

Boston moved into first place the last day of July and stayed there all of August and the first 18 days of September. Then the team dropped to second, and ultimately closed out by winning two of three from Chicago White Sox at Fenway (Brunansky making a game-saving catch) to clinch the pennant on the last day of the season. But Red Sox hopes for another shot at the World Series suffered badly from a shoulder injury that kept Clemens sidelined for much of September. Just as in 1988, the Sox lost four straight to Oakland, including a controversial fourth game when umpire Terry Cooney ejected Clemens in the second inning, claiming he had cursed at the umpire. Clemens denied it, but when he left, the flagging hopes of the team went with him, and Oakland got into the World Series (only to be beaten by Los Angeles).

Realizing that the team of the eighties had run down, the Sox went into the free agency market with a vengeance and a wide-open pocketbook. They signed Jack Clark, a slugging outfielder and first baseman who had played for San Francisco, St. Louis, the Yankees and San Diego: He got a four-year pact worth $3.5 million a year. Matt Young, a lefthander of questionable promise, signed a three-year deal with the Sox at $2.5 million a year. Then the team went out and spent $3 million-plus a season for Danny Darwin, who had pitched for the Texas Rangers. All three would prove to be very expensive failures for Boston.

That was because 1991 did not turn out the way the Red Sox brass had planned. Darwin was out most of the season with an arm injury. Matt Young went 3-7 with a 5.18 ERA and missed two months with an arm injury. He is best remembered—and disliked—by Red Sox fans as the reliever who came in for the 10th inning in a tie game against the Yankees at Fenway Park when the Sox were just a half game out of first. The team had won 18 of 22, including four in a row. Young walked three, and the Yanks won 7-5. The Sox lost 10 of the last 13 games, ending in a tie for second with Detroit, while Toronto won the division. The Sox had only two .300 hitters—Boggs at .332 and Greenwell at an even .300. Clark hit .249 but had a team-leading 28 home runs and a team high 87 RBIs—also a team-high 133 strikeouts. Roger Clemens went 18-10 with a 2.62 ERA and won the Cy Young Award for the third time.

Overall, the 1991 Red Sox record of 84-78 was not bad, but it signaled the start of a Boston slide that carried through 1992, 1993 and 1994. The 1992 season began with a lot of changes at the top. First Jean R. Yawkey, widow of the late Red Sox owner Thomas A. Yawkey, died. She had been the majority general partner, the one who made the major decisions after her husband died in 1976. John Harrington, president of the Red Sox and long affiliated with the Yawkeys, took over as chief executive officer of the team. That ended 59 years of Yawkey ownership.

The next shakeup came with the firing of Joe Morgan, who had won 301 games and lost 262. His teams won the AL East two of his four years as manager, and the other two teams ended in second and third place. It was a record that would look good on most managerial resumes, but evidently not good enough for the Red Sox. There was the feeling that Morgan managed by instinct rather than by logic. He was replaced by Butch Hobson, the former Red Sox third baseman who had managed the top Sox farm team, Pawtucket, to an International League championship. Harrington also dug into the Red Sox's deep pocket and signed left-hander Frank Viola as a free agent, paying him $4.5 million a year for three years.

It was all for naught, because the 1992 season was a disaster. The Sox never got any higher than fourth place and ended up at 73-89, last place in the AL East. There was not a single .300 hitter, not even Wade Boggs, whose .259 placed him below .300 for the first time in his big-league career. Clemens had another good year, 18-11, and led the league in ERA at 2.41 and shutouts with five. He missed the last six games because of an arm injury. Darwin finally pitched a full season but went 9-9, and Viola was 13-

12. Despite all this, the team drew 2,468,574 fans to Fenway Park.

The Red Sox clearly had some problems, and they went out to correct them for 1993. Perhaps the biggest shock came when they let go of Wade Boggs, who wanted a four-year contract at $4 million-per, while the Sox offered only $3 million-per for two years. They went into free agency and got Andre Dawson, who had a Hall of Fame career with Montreal and the Cubs. Now, at 38, with two very bad knees, he signed a two-year deal with the Sox at $4 million a year. Boston hoped he would supply the punch that had been lacking in its lineup. But Dawson missed 35 games with knee injuries and was hobbled in many of the games in which he played; he ended up with a .273 average, with 13 homers and 67 RBIs.

The Sox gave up on Jack Clark, paid him his salary for the third year and released

Tom (Flash) Gordon became a reliable closer, with 46 saves in 1988.

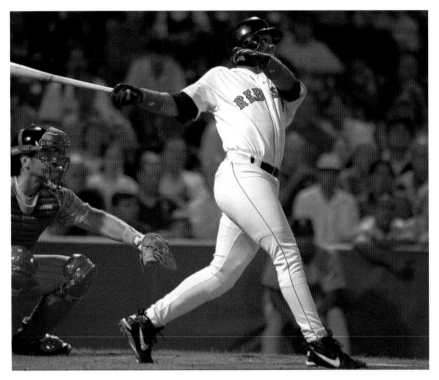

Left: *Troy O'Leary's walk-off homer beat Minnesota 11-10 in 1996.*

Right: *Shortstop Nomar Garciaparra (1996-2004) was one of the most popular players in Red Sox history.*

him. The Sox also parted company with Jeff Reardon, who had by then become the all-time major league save leader with his 354. Also departing was Jody Reed, who could not come to terms with the Sox and ended up in Los Angeles for less money than he had been offered in Boston. Mo Vaughn, who had been demoted to Pawtucket the year before, came back with a .297 average with 29 homers and 101 RBIs. Scott Cooper, now the regular third baseman with Boggs off to the Yankees, hit .279 and was the only Red Sox rep on the AL All-Star team. Clemens, pitching with a strained groin muscle, had his first sub .500 season, going 11-14. Viola finished 11-8 but needed elbow surgery at the end of the season. Darwin, finally producing as the Sox had hoped, led the team with a 15-11 season. Despite their shortcomings, the Sox made a race of it for awhile. They went on a 9-0 tear late in July, actually moved into first place and remained in contention until late in August when they dropped six back. They ended the season with six consecutive losses, to finish at 80-82 and end up in fifth place, 15 behind the champion Blue Jays.

It was clearly time for some basic changes. John Harrington began by replacing General Manager Lou Gorman with Dan Duquette, the Amherst College graduate who had built the Montreal Expos into one of the better teams in baseball. Duquette (like Reardon, a native of Dalton, Massachusetts) joined the Sox in January 1994 amid great hopes for big changes, but he took his time, waiting to see just what the Red Sox had and what they needed. The Sox started the '94 season with a rush, setting a team record with 17 wins in April. They were still in first

place on May 8 with a 20-7 mark, but already things were slipping. On opening day, Greenwell had crashed into the fence in left and injured a shoulder that hampered his swing the rest of the season. Viola tore his left elbow in early May and was out for the season. Dawson started strongly but his knees acted up again and he missed part of the season. Clemens remained a force, but the team got him few runs and he ended with a 9-7 record and a 2.85 ERA, second best in the AL. By June 1, the Sox were 31-19, only 2 ½ back in second place. They went on an 11-game losing streak and never recovered, ending at 54-61, in fourth place, 17 games back of the Yankees, who led the AL East with baseball's best record when the strike came August 18.

Once Commissioner Bud Selig announced on September 14 that the remainder of the season and the playoffs had been canceled, 1994 became the game's darkest year since the 1919 Black Sox scandal. The Red Sox could not claim that they were derailed from a championship, but both the players and management suffered like everyone else in the major leagues from the angry repercussions of fans and media.

Independent of the work stoppage, the Red Sox front office fired Manager Butch Hobson and hired Kevin Kennedy from the Texas Rangers. Over the winter, Andre Dawson and Scott Cooper left the team, but many new faces arrived. By the time the players and owners agreed on April 2 to start the 1995 season 23 days later, only Roger Clemens and Mike Greenwell remained from the 1986 American League champions. Joining Clemens in the rotation were new acquisitions Zane Smith (from Pittsburgh),

Erik Hanson (Cincinnati) and Rheal Cormier (St. Louis). Another Cardinal, Luis Alicea, moved to second base, and his teammate Mark Whiten was slated for center. Moreover, onetime American League MVP José Canseco, who had hit .769 at Fenway in '94, arrived from Texas in exchange for speedster Otis Nixon.

The new combination clicked almost instantly: The Sox led the East Division by three games at the halfway point, won 13 of 14 games in early August and coasted to their last divisional title, finishing seven games ahead of New York with an 86-58 record in the shortened season. If designated hitter Canseco (.306, 24, 81) didn't match his peak production, first baseman Mo Vaughn (.300, 39, 126) had an MVP year and shortstop Valentin (.298, 27, 102, 20 stolen bases) was an all-around threat. Valentin and Vaughn had grand slams in consecutive innings of an especially satisfying win over the Yankees. Although Clemens, who had

started the year with shoulder trouble, slipped to 10-5 with a 4.18 ERA, Hanson picked up the slack with a 15-5 record; Pittsburgh castoff Tim Wakefield (16-8) started 14-1 and had the league's second best ERA at 2.95; and Rick Aguilera, a July 6 pickup from Minnesota, finished all 30 of his games and saved 20 of them. Unfortunately, Boston's opponent in the first round of the playoffs was Cleveland, widely considered the best team in baseball. After a spirited opener that went 13 innings before the Indians won 5-4, the Sox were swept in three games, with Vaughn and Canseco going 0-for-27.

The 1996 season certainly had its individual highlights. Roger Clemens tied his major league record by fanning 20 Tigers on September 18, Vaughn had another gargantuan (.326, 44, 143) All-Star season and newcomer Heathcliff Slocumb saved 31 games and made everyone's all-name team. Unfortunately, the Red Sox lost 19 of their

After a homer in 1998, Nomar Garciaparra (right) is congratulated by three other Boston bashers (from left)— John Valentin, Mo Vaughn and Troy O'Leary.

Bret Saberhagen, beating Detroit on September 11, 1998, won 15 games to prove he wasn't washed up.

first 25 games and finished third with an 85-77 record. They led the league in unearned runs. Since they were 1-11 against Cleveland, there wasn't much point in going to the post-season. Even so, home attendance increased over 1995, to 2.3 million.

One of many Sox pitchers who peaked after his Boston years, Aaron Sele went 7-11. Hanson had left for Toronto, Wakefield continued his disappointing late-'95 pace, and Tom Gordon only went 12-9 because his teammates supplied seven or more runs in all his wins. The staff yielded the second most walks. And Clemens? When he was 10-13 in his free-agent season, General Manager Duquette refused to bid for him, declaring famously that Roger was in the "twilight of his career." Clemens stayed in the American League another seven years and went 118-49 for the Blue Jays and Yankees. Duquette also dismissed Manager Kennedy—notwithstanding baseball's best record over the final two months—and replaced him with Jimy Williams, late of Toronto.

The 1996 season was just as notable for off-the-field problems. Owner John Harrington assigned an "impartial management consultant" to meet separately with the feuding Duquette and Williams. Red Sox veterans sided with Williams, and Duquette scarcely helped his case with his losing-means-you-never-have-to-say-you're sorry attitude. But someone had to take the blame for a powerful but defensively porous club that *Sports Illustrated* called a "slo-pitch softball team."

The 1997 Red Sox never got over the loss of Clemens or the surgeries of Vaughn and Naehring, finishing fourth with a 78-84 record. Steve Avery, twice a 19-game winner, was penciled in as Clemens's replace-

ment, but he went 6-7, with a 6.42 ERA and 178 baserunners in 96 ⅔ innings. Sele (13-12) and Wakefield (12-15) never looked like stoppers, and minutes before the July 31 midnight trading deadline closer Slocumb (0-5, 17 saves, 5.79 ERA) was traded to Seattle for two little-noted players, catcher Jason Varitek and pitcher Derek Lowe. As the Sox used innumerable new faces like catcher Scott Hatteberg, outfielder Darren Bragg and designated hitter Reggie Jefferson, shortstop Nomar Garciaparra hit .306, with 30 homers and 98 RBIs in his first full season. When Nomar broke Johnny Pesky's team record for rookie hits with 209, Duquette typically neglected to invite the old Sox employee to see him make history in Toronto. Emblematic of this lost season was the presence of leftfielder Wil Cordero, who was arrested for hitting his wife with a telephone, was booed daily and finally dispatched to the White Sox at season's end.

Say this for the modern era of free agency and arbitration: Rapid turnover can make also-rans into instant winners. Who could imagine that the '97 losers would be play-off-bound a year later? Signed to a six-year, $75 million contract as a free agent, former Expo Pedro Martinez went 19-7, had a 2.89 ERA and won the Cy Young Award. With a bona fide stopper in hand, the Red Sox took seven straight in April and five of their last six decisions, finished 92-70 and qualified as the American League's wild card team. Wakefield (17-8) and Comeback Player of the Year Bret Saberhagen (15-8) were energized by Martinez's leadership. Vaughn (.337, 40, 115) and Garciaparra (.323, 35, 122) provided more than enough offense, and .272-hitting second baseman Mike Benjamin proved to be a bargain at his $242,500 salary. On his part, curveballer Gordon closed games so effectively and evidently so touchingly, with 46 saves, that Stephen King later wrote a novel called *The Girl Who Loved Tom Gordon*.

There were only brief heroics, however, in the post-season. While the otherworldly Yankees (114-48) dusted off Texas in one divisional playoff, the Red Sox faced their nemesis Indians. In the divisional series opener, Martinez bested the Indians 11-3 in the opener and silenced the crowd at Cleveland's Jacobs Field. The Sox seemed headed for another win, after they led 2-0 in the first, and Cleveland Manager Mike Hargrove and pitcher Dwight Gooden were already dismissed by home plate umpire Joe Brinkman. A better team would have jumped at the opportunity, but Wakefield barely lasted longer than Gooden and was sacked for five runs in 1 ⅓ innings in a 9-5 loss. In Game 3, Saberhagen yielded three homers—1,186 feet of longball, a maddeningly fastidious

Boston scribe reported—to fall behind 3-1. "I needed to be a ground-ball pitcher today," Saberhagen said. "I was a fly-ball pitcher. That was the story of the game." Well almost. Relieving in the last appearance of his Hall of Fame career, Dennis Eckersley threw a home-run ball to Manny Ramirez in the ninth. That put Cleveland up 4-1, and Garciaparra's two-run blast left the Sox one run short.

With the Sox season on the line, Manager Williams took heat for starting Pete Schourek in do-or-die Game 4 rather than re-using Martinez on only three days' rest. The gamble almost worked. Schourek made Williams look good by allowing only two hits and no runs, leaving after 5 ⅓ innings with the Sox up 1-0 on a Nomah homah. With a chance to go up by two, third base Coach Wendell Kim unwisely waved in Valentin from second on a sixth-inning single to left and he was easily thrown out. Replacing Schourek, Lowe retired five straight before Williams again tempted fate. This time he used Tom Gordon to start the eighth inning for the first time in 1998. Alas, Gordon gave up three straight hits, including leftfielder David Justice's two-run double and lost 2-1. Afterward, Nomar, who set a divisional-series record with 11 RBIs, stood in front of the Red Sox dugout asking the fans to cheer. "We want Mo!" they chorused, referring not to momentum but Mo Vaughn, who would soon be taking his own 8 postseason RBIs to Anaheim.

Still, the 1999 Red Sox did not disappoint. His career numbers eerily resembling those of Hall of Famer Sandy Koufax, Martinez went 23-4, with a 2.07 ERA and helped the Red Sox lead the league with a team ERA of 4.00. Opponents couldn't pitch around Nomar, because Troy O'Leary (103 RBIs) was batting behind him. As a result, Garciaparra won the batting title—a relatively rare feat for a righthanded hitter—with a .357 average. Former Dodger Jose Offerman (.294) and new rightfielder Trot Nixon (.270, 15 homers) gave the Red Sox a balanced offense. Give that man Duquette credit when he deserved it: The two no-names for whom he traded Heathcliff Slocumb back in 1997 were paying off in more ways than one. Catcher Varitek (.269, 20, 76) and pitcher Lowe (6-3, 2.63, 15 saves), both making under $300,000, were among the best bargains in baseball. It all added up to a 94-68 season, a second-place finish four games behind the Yanks and another wild-card berth.

But could the Red Sox finally unseat the Indians in a divisional playoff? Longtime Red Sox observers wrote them off as soon as Martinez left the opener with a back strain after four innings, Valentin made a

two-out throwing error and Lowe immediately surrendered a two-run homer to Jim Thome. The Indians won, 3-1 after Lowe plunked Ramirez to lead off the ninth— never, never put the leadoff hitter on—and Travis Fryman hit a bases-loaded single. The cynics circled. Before Game 2, ESPN's Peter Pascarelli saw Shaughnessy at the batting cage. "Pedro is now day-to-day, and Red Sox fans are century-to-century," Pascarelli said.

Whereupon the Indians unloaded on Saberhagen and won Game 2, 11-1. "As Usual, October Outlook Is Grim," read a *Boston Globe* headline. The Red Sox faced Game 3 without Garciaparra, who had a wrist injury. With the score tied at 3-3 in the seventh and an Indian on base courtesy of another Valentin error, Lowe again faced Thome. How grim could things get? This time Lowe froze him with an inside fastball. This time Valentin's two-run double ignited a six-run, seventh inning rally. This time the Red Sox won, 9-3. But who remembers the great moments in Red Sox history?

Ignited by Valentin's two-run homer and 7 RBIs, the Red Sox won Game 4, 23-7, and set series records for most runs and the

Up-and-down Derek Lowe saved his best stuff for the biggest games, including the World Series finale in 2004.

No Red Sox pitcher ever approached Pedro Martinez's .760 win percentage for 1998-2004.

another cover jinx. So you think pitching wins pennants? Pedro went 18-6 record with a see-it-to-believe it 1.74 ERA, with his brother Ramon adding 10 more wins, and the staff again led the league in ERA. Moreover, Lowe kept the Sox in the race with 42 saves, and he was ably set up by a cast that included the portly Rich Garces. "El Guapo" (Handsome Man) allowed just 64 hits and 23 walks in 74 ⅔ innings.

Everyday players offered a mixed bag. They gave Pedro seven runs to work with in his six losses. Third base, first base and designated hitter lacked their expected power production. Second baseman Offerman's defensive lapses seemed more glaring when his average slipped to .255. Newcomer Carl "Dr. Evil" Everett signed a three-year, $21 million contract, played a mean centerfield and struck fear in opposing pitchers' hearts with his three-pronged (.300, 34, 108) hitting, but he was even nastier in the clubhouse. The time bomb would explode a year later. The Sox moved edgily through an 85-77 year.

The 2001 Red Sox (82-79) were lucky to finish over .500. Pedro's shoulder injury limited him to 18 games, and Nomar missed almost the whole season with wrist problems. A trio of new pitchers, Hideo Nomo (13-10), Frank Castillo (10-9) and David Cone (9-7) pitched manfully in Pedro's absence, and free-agent acquisition Manny Ramirez had his usual Jimmie Foxx season when he hit .306, with 41 homers and 125 runs batted in. The Sox needed him desperately, because the slumping, ailing Everett (.257, 14, 58) missed a team bus in March and plainly outstayed his welcome. But the real culprit was Duquette. The team was magically three games out of a playoff slot in August, when he fired Williams, whom he had undermined in a dispute with Everett. Granted, Williams didn't communicate with the players and confused them with ever-changing lineups, but he was the winningest manager fired in mid-season since Billy Martin in 1988. The Sox went 17-26 under Williams's successor Joe Kerrigan (pitching coaches are notoriously poor managers) and finished 13 ½ games back. In September, Duquette added injury to insult when he insisted that Pedro pitch. Martinez lasted three innings and was done for the season with a tear in his rotator cuff.

Duquette was finally fired on February 28, 2002, the day John Henry and his associates took over the Red Sox from John Harrington. Almost immediately, the new owners replaced Kerrigan with Oakland bench coach Grady Little, and the players greeted him with a standing ovation. Martinez went 20-4, Lowe made an excellent (21-8) transition to starter and Ugueth

largest margin of victory by a winner. The deciding fifth game couldn't possibly be so easy. It wasn't. With the Red Sox leading a slugfest 8-7 after three innings (Saberhagen and Lowe having been lit up), Martinez limbered up his back and took over. All he did was pitch six innings of no-hit relief, biding his time until Troy O'Leary's second home run of the game won it, 12-8.

Unfortunately, Pedro's fireworks, like so much of the good in Red Sox history, were little noted nor long remembered. The Yankees took care of that in the ALCS. New York's Bernie Williams won the opener, 4-3 on a 10th inning homer, and the Yankees took Game 2, 3-2 as the Red Sox went 1-for-12 with runners in scoring position and missed two homers by inches. The 1999 Sox could only go to the well once, and they lost the best-of-seven series in five. In the end, things got ugly. Nomar misplayed six different balls, Williams lost his composure protesting a bad call while Fenway fans threw debris on the field, and a security operative swore at the Yankee players he was assigned to protect.

In 2000–2002, the Red Sox repeated in second place, but failed to get wild-card slots. It was another millennium, but age-old problems reappeared. *Sports Illustrated* picked Boston to win it all in 2000; chalk it up to

Urbina added 40 saves. But as Bill Chuck of Billy-Ball.com put it, Red Sox pitching hopes rested inordinately in "Pedro and Lowe and pray for snow."

Johnny Damon (late of Oakland) and Rickey Henderson (late of everywhere) joined the club; the former added speed and savvy in center, while the latter showed his advancing age. A twenty-something, new General Manager Theo Epstein looked for players who could go long in the count and reach base often, though third baseman Shea Hillenbrand had only 25 walks in 676 plate appearances. The first base pretenders, notably Tony Clark (.207), were baseball's worst. Even so, the Red Sox went 93-69 and contested for a wild-card slot until the bitter end.

Things had to improve in 2003, and they did. Though Casey Fossum didn't develop into the starter they were counting on and a bullpen-by-committee busted early, the Sox got their wild-card wish (finishing second as usual behind the Yanks). Epstein boldly traded Hillenbrand for Arizona's Byung-Hyun Kim, who converted 16 of 19 save opportunities. What's more, Kid Theo got the patient hitters he craved in first baseman-designated hitter David Ortiz (4.13 pitches per at-bat in 2002) and versatile Kevin Millar (3.99). Ortiz was an MVP candidate, and Millar set the clubhouse tone when he urged his teammates to "cowboy up." This western term describes a rider who re-mounts after being thrown by his horse, and it inspired the Sox to kick off adversity. No one got the message better than the manager. When Ramirez refused to pinch-hit in Philadelphia, Little benched him for a game, earning the team's respect.

The Red Sox began the divisional series against Oakland cowboy down. Kim immediately blew two saves in two losses, cashiering him for the year, and the Red Sox only won Game 3 because the A's gave it away. The next do-or-die contest was uncomfortably close until Ortiz grabbed it with a two-run double off Oakland closer Keith Foulke. Finally, Martinez beat the A's 4-3 in the deciding game. Pressed back into bullpen service, Lowe froze the last two batters on strike three.

Let's fast-forward through the first six games of the league championship series that split with the Yankees, pausing only in Game 3. Having already blown a 2-0 lead, Martinez plunked Karim Garcia near his ear in the third inning, then pointed at his own head in a shouting match with Yankee catcher Jorge Posada as if to say "You're next." As players on both clubs agreed, throwing at a batter's head is disgraceful. In the fourth, New York's Roger Clemens threw high and inside but not especially close to Ramirez's head. Manny pointlessly started toward the mound, both benches emptied and Martinez warded off a charge from the Yankees' 72-year-old bench coach Don Zimmer by tossing him to the ground. What's more, a Sox employee assigned to the Yankee bullpen came to blows with two Yankees when they accused him of rooting for the Sox.

Boston's ugly behavior could only lead to a bad end. Everyone from Bangor to Bridgeport knows what happened in Game 7. Martinez led the Yankees by three runs after seven innings, but he was plainly struggling. When Pedro reported to the mound in the eighth, consternation ruled throughout New England. Grannies in northern New Hampshire threw off their afghans. Boys up past their bedtime turned to their parents for explanation. "Take Pedro out!" everyone bellowed at their TVs. But Pedro stayed in. The Yankees tied the score and Sox fans broiled over hot stoves all winter once the Yankees' Aaron Boone ended their season with an 11th-inning homer off Wakefield.

Blowing a three-run lead in the league playoffs certainly didn't match losing in '86 after creeping to within one strike of a world championship. On the other hand, *The Curse of the Bambino* hadn't been written back then. In the aftermath of the 2003 letdown, Boston fans felt cursed for all time.

The Yankees' Aaron Boone homered off Tim Wakefield to end Red Sox hopes in 2003.

13. Lowering the Curtain on Tragedy

I n the 86 years between championships, Red Sox history resembled a Shakespearean tragedy, complete with high station, hubris, ruin, catharsis and reversal. It was only fitting that the season of salvation should begin in a spirit of desperation and disillusionment.

ACT I: THE PRE-SEASON

Alas, poor world, what treasure hast thou lost!

—Venus and Adonis

Scene 1: Off-season, 2003–2004. The Red Sox think they have acquired Texas short-stop Alex Rodriguez, widely considered the game's best all-around player, in an off-season trade for the disgraced Manny Ramirez and cash. In a related deal, the Sox expect to trade shortstop Nomar Garciaparra to the White Sox for outfielder Magglio Ordoñez. The Rodriguez swap is all but signed and sealed when the Players Association—of all groups—vetoes it because A-Rod would have to take a pay cut. When he subsequently is traded to the hated Yankees, a cold New England fall and winter turn damp as

Top right: *Ace acquisition Curt Schilling and team leader, catcher Jason Varitek, confer during the 2004 season.*

Below: *Varitek tags out the Yankees' Hideki Matsui during the American League Championship Series.*

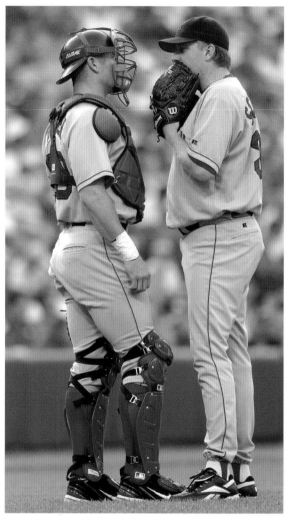

well. It hardly helps that the untraded Garciaparra, who will become a free agent in November, makes no secret of his interest in leaving.

Nonetheless, the off-season is profitable. The Sox replace manager Grady Little with Oakland bench coach Terry Francona. General Manager Theo Epstein spends Thanksgiving negotiating at the home of Arizona pitcher Curt Schilling and gets him to waive his no-trade clause and then sign a contract that includes a $2 million bonus and a $13 million extension for 2007 if Boston wins the 2004 World Series. A big reason Schilling joins the Sox is that Francona managed him in Philadelphia. And Boston acquires a reliable reliever (for a change) in Oakland's Keith Foulke. Still, a now-or-never aura settles over the approach-

ing 2004 season, because almost half the players will become free agents afterward. Among them are Garciaparra, designated hitter and first baseman David Ortiz, and pitchers Pedro Martinez and Derek Lowe—not to mention the redoubtable catcher Jason Varitek.

Scene 2: Spring training. Hardly auspicious. Garciaparra and rightfielder Trot Nixon suffer disabling injuries, and Foulke's ineffectiveness sends a shiver through the front office.

ACT II: THE SEASON

For sufferance is the badge of all our tribe.
—The Merchant of Venice

Scene 1: Spring. As if to confirm bad tidings, Martinez loses the opener. Nonetheless, the Sox go 15-6 in April! In Game 2, Schilling grabs the first of his 21 wins and Foulke the first of his 32 saves. Manny Ramirez becomes an American citizen and an extrovert.

All this happiness, so alien to the New England psyche, can't last. Third baseman Bill Mueller needs knee surgery; Garciaparra and Nixon, respectively, miss the first 57 and 63 games of the season; second baseman Mark Bellhorn slumps at bat and afield; and Boston settles into a long stretch of .500 ball (26-26 after May 1), although Ortiz does sign a two-year, $11.75 million contract and a $7.75 million option for 2007.

Men at some time are masters of their fate.
—Julius Caesar

Scene 2: Mid-summer. Something has to give. With the Sox trailing the Yankees by nine games on July 24 amid worry that they'll drop out of the wild-card race, they fight back—literally. A-Rod complains about being hit in the arm by Boston's Bronson Arroyo, so the 6'2", 230-pound Varitek sticks a glove in his face, touching off a Fenway fracas. Tempers cool, and the Yankees take their customary lead. But with the Sox trailing 10-9 and one out in the ninth, Mueller hits a two-run homer off a longtime Red Sox nemesis, Yankee closer Mariano Rivera.

Red Sox players call the incident a turning point. Of equal importance, a week later, Epstein trades "Nomah," one of the franchise's all-time popular players, to the Cubs in a four-team, eight-player deal that lands two gold glovers, Montreal shortstop Orlando Cabrera and Minnesota first baseman Doug Mientkiewicz. In another move, the Sox get Los Angeles outfielder Dave Roberts, one of baseball's top base-stealers.

As much as anyone, the manager propels Boston forward. Risking censure, Francona starts Mientkiewicz at second on August 16; the Sox win and take 20 of 22 to control the wild-card race. For the most part, Mientkiewicz, Roberts and second baseman Pokey Reese are specialty bench men, but no one is complaining.

We have heard the chimes at midnight.
—Henry IV, Part 2

Left: *Manny Ramirez had three singles and two errors in the opening game of 2004 World Series, but the Sox won 11-9.*

Below: *David Ortiz celebrates his game-winning hit in Game 5 of the ALCS with the Yankees.*

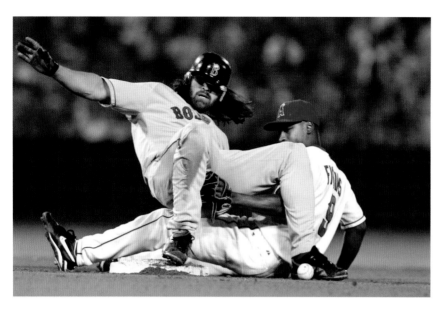

Top: *Johnny Damon knocks over Anaheim's Chone Figgins while stealing 2nd base in Game 2 of the American League Division Series.*

Below: *Keith Foulke saved Game 1 of the World Series against the Cardinals.*

Scene 3: The Boston clubhouse. About the long-haired, bearded Johnny Damon, *Sports Illustrated's* Rick Reilly writes, "How can you not love a team whose centerfielder looks like he was called up from the farm club at Bethlehem?" How can you not love the laid-back Francona, who tells Damon to grow his hair longer still if he likes? And how can you not love the three Dominican dandies: paterfamilias Ortiz, known to one and all by the Spanish term "Papí," plus Martinez and Ramirez with their Cabbage Patch Kids hairdos? Indeed, there are more varieties of hair facial and otherwise, including Arroyo's cornrows and Lowe's mullet,

than you'd find at a collection of Hell's Angels. In marked contrast to the "25 guys, 25 cabs" Sox of yore, the players fraternize and gambol in wide-eyed delight like boys playing a man's game. Come to think of it, that's what many of them are. Mobbed at the plate after a walk-off home run, Cabrera says later, "The whole time, somebody was trying to pull my pants down!" No wonder the players call themselves "idiots."

But don't get the impression the Sox aren't serious. The short-haired, stolid Varitek is a no-nonsense team leader: backbone and backstop, as one writer puts it. Schilling pitches in pain all season with a sore right ankle and soldiers on after suffering a ruptured sheath around the ankle-stabilizing peroneal tendon. All the while, he's blogging with fans and fund-raising for ALS (Lou Gehrig's Disease) research. In outfielder Gabe Kapler and third baseman Kevin Youkilis, the club has two Jewish strongmen from the tradition of Samson, Youkilis doubling as the Greek God of Walks. But the players are all of one mind, because they agree on what matters most—rings, the World Series variety.

Boston finishes the regular season in second place for the seventh year in a row, their 98-64 record easily qualifying for the American League's wild-card spot (the fourth time in those same years). Ramirez and Ortiz become the first American Leage pair since Babe Ruth and Lou Gehrig to accumulate 40 homers, 130 runs batted in and a .300 average apiece. You could do worse—you could hardly do better—than a one-two pitching punch of Schilling (21-6) and Martinez (16-9), even if Martinez famously calls the Yankees "my daddy" after losing to them on September 24. Cabrera scoops up grounders like a mother cradling a baby. Roberts can steal bases in his sleep.

ACT III: THE POST-SEASON

Neither rhyme nor reason.
                              —*As You Like It*

Scene 1: The divisional series. All in all, a team to be reckoned with. Except, presumably, in the post-season. The past hangs heavy. No World Series wins since 1918. Seven-game losses in the 1946, 1967, 1975 and 1986 fall classics. One-game pennant playoff losses to Cleveland (1948) and New York (1978). Division and league championship defeats you don't even want to think of. And it seems The Curse will forever spook the Red Sox. Though ballplayers are notably deficient in baseball history, all the current Sox know about Bill Buckner. No one wants to be the next designated goat.

So they sail into the playoffs, boats against

the current. First up, in the best-of-five divisional series: the California Angels, world champions in 2002. Pitching and fielding often make the difference in the post-season, and the October 5 opener is no exception. Angels manager Mike Scoscia uses his best defensive lineup, a move that backfires when third baseman Chone Figgins throws wildly to home, and the Red Sox go on to score five unearned runs in the fourth inning. Meanwhile, Schilling, who enters the game with a 5-1 record and 1.66 ERA in 11 previous postseason games, pitches 7 ⅔ productive innings for a 9-3 win.

The following day Martinez (0-4, 7.72 ERA in October) lasts seven strong innings (Francona knows when to relieve him), allowing three runs on six hits, in an 8-3 win. Ramirez breaks a 3-3 tie with a seventh-inning sacrifice fly off Francisco Rodriguez, and the Sox score four times in the ninth against reliever Brendan Donnelly. "Boston…won against one of the best bullpens in baseball," Scoscia says. For their part, Red Sox relievers Mike Timlin, Mike Myers and Foulke retire six of seven batters.

The series resumes in Boston on October 8. You can throw out the pitching-and-fielding scenario in Fenway's comfy confines. Notwithstanding Arroyo's five-run lead, the game goes into overtime when Vladimir Guerrero's seventh-inning grand slam ties the score at 6-6. Lowe, who has struggled so badly during the season that he's been relegated to the bullpen, works out of a first-and-third jam in the 10th. With Johnny Damon on first and two outs in the Sox half, Scoscia summons Game 1 loser Jarrod Washburn to face Ortiz in a lefty-on-lefty match-up. Señor

Octubre, as Hall-of-Famer Reggie Jackson calls him, hits the first pitch over the Green Monster, and the 8-6 winners are headed into the pennant playoffs. In a jubilant post-game celebration, Martinez and first baseman Kevin Millar do a victory lap while spraying champagne into the stands.

Some men are born great, some achieve greatness, and some have greatness thrust upon them.
                                  —*Twelfth Night*

Scene 2: The league championship series. All well and good, but the Sox now have to play the Yankees in the American League Championship Series. More ghosts, more demons: Jerry Coleman's pop double to ruin Boston's '49 season, Bucky Dent's homer in the '78 playoff, Aaron Boone's walk-off blast in 2003.

This time, it seems, the pain will be brief. In the best-of-seven LCS, the Yankees win Games 1 (10-7), 2 (3-1) and 3 (19-8!) and stand three outs from the World Series with

Left: *Red Sox Manager Terry Francona concentrates during Game 4 of the World Series.*

Below: *Key mid-season acquisition shortstop Orlando Cabrera solidified what had been a suspect defense.*

As generous as they were jubilant in victory, the Red Sox voted full shares of World Series money to 58 Boston personnel and were named "Sportsmen of the Year" by Sports Illustrated.

Following Page:
Reliever Keith Foulke and first baseman Doug Mientkiewicz celebrate after the last out of the 2004 World Series.

that man Rivera on the mound to hold a 4-3 lead. Now the full horror of Red Sox frustrations settle over Fenway: a hundred indecisions, a hundred visions and revisions, Denny Galehouse losing the '48 pennant playoff, the team failing to sign a black player until 1959, Luis Aparicio stumbling after rounding third in '72, and more. Club president Larry Lucchino is preparing a concession statement. Fans contemplate turning attention to the presidential race. Only an idiot could harbor any hope for the Soxies.

But that's what the Red Sox are, by their own gleeful admission. A cynic sees darkness in the tunnel. The Idiots see starts by Martinez and Schilling, if they can just get to Rivera. Millar walks to start the ninth and is immediately replaced by pinch runner Roberts. After several pickoff attempts, Roberts barely steals second. If he'd failed, the ever-inclusive Francona says later, the season probably would have sputtered out. As it is, Mueller singles Roberts home, and Rivera has blown just the fourth of 36 postseason save attempts.

With the game in extra innings, the Sox escape narrowly in the 11th, when Curtis Leskanic retires Bernie Williams on a bases-loaded fly, and in the 12th, when Leskanic fans Miguel Cairo with a runner on second. Then Ramirez singles, and Ortiz hits another walk-off homer, this one into the rightfield bullpen. Ortiz dances into his teammates' arms at the plate. "We always find a way to make it hard on ourselves," Lowe says. Idiots, the lot of them.

Still, no team has come from three games down to win in October, and only the greatest comeback in sports history will do it. Game 4 has lasted five hours, two minutes, leaving just 15 hours to rest before an afternoon tilt on Monday, October 18. And that game takes 14 innings, five hours and 49 minutes.

Six outs from elimination and trailing 4-2 this time, the Sox tie the score in the eighth on Ortiz's leadoff homer off Tom Gordon and Varitek's sacrifice fly off the star-crossed Rivera. Six innings of unbelievable tension follow, while Timlin, Foulke, Arroyo, Myers, Alan Embree and Tim Wakefield run the Boston bullpen's scoreless streak to 14 ⅓ innings. At one point, Timlin faces Rodriguez with a man on third and one out. Getting a man in from third with fewer than two outs is an article of faith in baseball; with a solid if unspectacular season, A-Rod has more to prove than most. Timlin fans the faux Red Sox on a two-seam fastball up and in.

At the top of the 13th, the dam is ready to break. Unaccountably, knuckleballer Wakefield works with Varitek instead of his personal catcher Doug Mirabelli. Wakefield strikes out leadoff hitter Gary Sheffield, but his knuckler floats away from Varitek and Sheffield reaches base. Two more passed balls put runners on second and third. Another knuckler gets away from Varitek—another season twisting and bouncing away?—but it remains in front of the plate to hold baserunners in place. Finally, Wakefield fans Ruben Sierra on a 70-mph knuckler.

Red Sox fans cheer on players as they pass by during Boston's rolling rally in celebration of the team's World Series championship.

In the Sox 14th Damon and Ramirez walk. Up steps Papí with two outs—who else could it be?—to foul off six pitches (one almost a homer to right), then to bloop the game's 471st pitch to center, scoring Damon. Sox win 5-4! New York still leads the series three games to two, and action now shifts to Yankee Stadium, but the whole world puts the Red Sox in the catbird seat. "This team has done something in the last two days that will go down in history as an incredible accomplishment," says the avuncular Kapler.

"Hating the New York Yankees is as American as apple pie, unwed mothers and cheating on your income tax," the Chicago columnist Mike Royko once wrote. But the Red Sox have little room for hatred, which would distract them. Coolly, resolutely, with his tendon sutured and blood seeping through his right sock, Schilling silences the Yankees and their 55,000 fans in a 4-2 Game 6 masterpiece. There are some tense moments, to be sure. After Cabrera singles home a run in the fourth, Bellhorn's hit over the leftfield wall is ruled a ground-rule double. When Francona complains, the umpires huddle and reverse the call, giving Bellhorn a homer and putting the Red Sox up 4-0. And in the eighth, after Jeter cuts the lead to 4-2 with a run-scoring single, Rodriguez hits a nubber between the mound and first. Arroyo fields it and tries to tag the runner, but Rodriguez slaps the ball out of his glove, so Jeter scores all the way from first. Another complaint. Another huddled umpires' conference. Another reversed call rules Rodriguez out for interference, and Jeter returns to first. After a 10-minute delay in which fans shower the

field with debris and Yankee manager Joe Torre disputes the call in vain, play resumes, and the Red Sox win, 4-2.

Noted head case Derek Lowe starts Game 7. No matter. Pitching on only two days' rest, he keeps his sinker down to allow only one hit in six innings. When Johnny Damon delivers two homers and Papí yet another one, Boston wins 10-3. No late-inning hysterics. No controversies. Just total domination.

"All empires fall sooner or later," Lucchino, who once called the Yankees "the evil empire," said.

"That's for the '03 team, just like it's for the '78 team and the '49 team," says Epstein. "I hope Ted Williams is having a cocktail upstairs."

Here we will sit and let the sounds of music
Creep in our ears; soft stillness and the night
Become the touches of sweet harmony.
—The Merchant of Venice

Scene 3: The World Series. The Curse is broken. Or is it? There is still the matter of the 86-year drought, the St. Louis Cardinals, their revered manager Tony La Russa, their jaw-dropping lineup and their friendly, knowledgeable fans standing between the Red Sox and their championship rings.

But the Sox, once cursed, suddenly grow blessed. Now, some will call the 2004 World Series anti-climactic. That's not fair. Having already staged the greatest comeback in post-season history, the Red Sox have earned an instant coronation. The four-game sweep in Boston and St. Louis is as good a time as any to start celebrating.

Game 1 is gutsy, entertaining, even funny. Though they lead 4-0, then 7-2, the Sox commit four errors and allow the Cardinals draw even at 7-7 and then 9-9. Their final two runs are gifts, courtesy of two consecutive eighth inning errors by Ramirez. First he bobbles a single, then he stumbles trying to make a sliding catch, so the ball ticks off his chest and rolls toward the left-field corner. Red Sox reserves crack up on the bench. In an AP writer's words, "Ramirez ran after balls as if he were trying to find them using Mapquest."

Enough foolishness. Bellhorn's two-run blast in the eighth gives the Red Sox a Raggedy Andy, 11-9 win. No one knows it, but the Series is as good as over. His tendon sutured in place and his ankle bleeding again, Schilling shuts down the Cardinals on four hits and one unearned run in six innings to win Game 2, 6-2. Not even another four Boston errors can keep it close. Scoring all their runs with two outs, the Idiots cross home on a rare Varitek triple, a Bellhorn double and a Cabrera single.

The Series switches to St. Louis. Pitching for free-agent bucks as well as the Red Sox, Martinez beats the Cards 4-1 in Game 3. Now the Red Sox really play like champions. Series MVP Ramirez (Bellhorn or Damon deserve the honor as much) throws out Larry Walker at the plate and Ortiz, playing first in a designated hitter-free game, nabs St. Louis pitcher Jeff Suppan hesitating between third and home. When Martinez leaves the game after seven innings, he and Ramirez rub hairy heads like two pussycats.

What's left for 52,037 Cardinal fans except to stand watching the Red Sox sweep on October 27. Johnny Damon opens the game with a homer for the only run the Red Sox will need. The one pitcher to win the last game of a divisional series, league championship series and World Series the same year, Lowe bests the Cardinals, 3-0. Fittingly, the last out is recorded on a comebacker to Foulke, who finishes every Series game. Like the total eclipse of the moon that occurs during the game, the Red Sox have eclipsed a record as winners of eight consecutive post-season games.

When Mientkiewicz squeezes Foulke's throw to first at 11:40 pm, church bells ring from Eastport to Block Island and Provincetown to Williamstown. Ancient fans can die happy. New England's cold climate and rocky soil transform into sun-splashed beaches.

During their 102 seasons in the major leagues, the Red Sox have fielded some of the game's best players: the winningest pitcher (Cy Young), the best pitcher (Roger Clemens or Lefty Grove), the best hitter (Ted Williams), the best player (Babe Ruth). With so much individual talent, so many tragic flaws and so much team failure, the 1919–2003 Sox are teams that enchant intellectuals and infuriate fans. Their lyric little bandbox of a ballpark lures righthanded sluggers slow afoot and clumsy afield. The Red Sox can swat homers against weak pitching, but they can't manufacture runs against strong pitching or keep the score down. Yet they always have heart. You gotta have heart.

Now all is right with their world. In the greatest celebration the 374-year-old Hub has ever seen, the Red Sox ride 17 amphibious "duck boats" through city streets and into the Charles River. The Curse is dead. The Sox can only surge ahead.

O brave new world,
That has such people in't!

—*The Tempest*

Pokey Reese, disabled and benched through much of the season, exemplifies Red Sox spirit as he jumps on teammates at end of the World Series.

14. Encore!

So we'll live,
And pray, and sing, and tell old tales,
and laugh
At gilded butterflies, and hear poor rogues
Talk of court news;
and we'll talk with them too—
Who loses and who wins;
who's in, who's out—

—*King Lear*

Just as Lear idealized a lifetime in prison because his beloved daughter Cordelia would be with him, so too could Red Sox fans bask in their championship like cats in sunlight. Where they once saw Fenway Park as a bleak house of false starts and dashed hopes, the faithful now thronged to the shrine to worship the championship banners with great expectations. Fans queued politely to touch the 2004 World Series trophy as it passed through villages and dells all over New England.

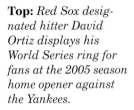

Top: *Red Sox designated hitter David Ortiz displays his World Series ring for fans at the 2005 season home opener against the Yankees.*

Right: *Dave Roberts, atop the shoulders of Mike Timlin, hoists the World Series trophy in celebration of the Sox sweep of St. Louis.*

The distractions proved useful. No Red Sox team had played in two consecutive World Series since 1916, and what demons awaited the 2005 club! Free-agent pitchers Pedro Martinez and Derek Lowe departed for the Mets and Dodgers, respectively. Curt Schilling, anchor of the 2004 rotation, returned too soon from ankle surgery and went 8-8, with 9 saves and a bloated 5.69 ERA. Closer Keith Foulke (15 saves, 5.91 ERA) also alternated between injured and ineffective. New shortstop Edgar Renteria led the majors with 30 errors.

Add 'em up: two stoppers gone, another crippled, a useless closer, a butterfingered shortstop. So how did the Red Sox (95-67) finish second for the eighth consecutive time and return for the post-season three years running?

No one loomed larger than David Ortiz, who nearly became the first designated hitter elected a league's Most Valuable Player when he batted .300, with 47 homers, a league-leading 148 runs batted in, a .604 slugging percentage and 88 extra-base hits. "Papí" was a fan favorite as well, something worth noting in a city once known for mistreating black athletes. Opponents couldn't pitch around Ortiz because Manny Ramirez (.292, 45, 144) waited on deck. Catcher Jason Varitek masterminded a mix-and-match rotation that got winning seasons from Bronson Arroyo (14-10) as well as newcomers Matt Clement (13-6) and David Wells (15-7). Backup Doug Mirabelli caught knuckle-baller Tim Wakefield (16-

12). Mike Timlin saved 13 games after Schilling and Foulke lapsed. And Johnny Damon (.316, 29-game hitting streak) produced as centerfielder and leadoff hitter in his free-agent year.

The season wasn't as dramatic as 2004—what could be?—but it had its moments. There was the Opening Day ring ceremony, in which popular favorites like Carlton Fisk and Carl Yastrzemski participated. The Sox and Devil Rays had their annual bench-clearing brawl. The nonstop drama of Manny being Manny continued. He came in like a lamb (for him) and out like a lion, as his late-season hitting helped stave off a wild-card bid by Cleveland. Only Manny could produce a game-winning RBI by being hit with a pitch. He made his seasonal demand to be shipped off, then a few hours after the trading deadline he drove in the winning run with a pinch-hit single. During a break in one game, he disappeared into a hole in the left-field wall. On another occasion, he let a ball go through his legs, fielded it off the wall, sidearmed a throw to nail a man at third and did a pirouette in the outfield.

The Sox were 46-35 in mid-season, sitting in first place after enjoying consecutive walk-off homers off Oakland by Kevin Millar and Varitek. Clement's 9-2 start earned him an All-Star berth. Naturally, he was hit on the head by a liner in Game 100 and pitched ineffectively down the stretch. As offense also declined in late-season, Ramirez and Ortiz were the one-two—and sometimes only—punch that kept the team going. Papí's game-tying homer and game-winning single in Game 159 pretty much

Left: *Catcher Jason Varitek follows a play at Wrigley Field during the 2005 regular season. Formerly bound in the misery of drought, the World Champion Red Sox and Cubs faced off for the first time since the 1918 World Series.*

Below: *Following the 2004 World Series win, the Sox looked to fill the hole left by Pedro Martinez's defection to the Mets with right-hander Matt Clement. In his first year with the Sox, Clement delivered a winning season and earned a trip to the All Star game with a 9 and 2 record at the break.*

iced the Indians. Typically, the Yankees won the division at Fenway. The Sox and Yankees actually finished in a dead heat, but the Yanks were deemed titlists, because they won the season series 10-9.

Boston was immediately swept by the White Sox in a food-for-thought divisional series. Jose Contreras shut down Red Sox bats in Chicago's 14-2 opening win. Then second baseman Tony Graffanino's error kept a Chicago rally alive, and the White Sox won Game 2, 5-4. Finally, after load-

Red Sox General Manager Theo Epstein welcomes shortstop Edgar Renteria for the 2005 season. Both Epstein and Renteria had a rough 2005 season; the shortstop leading the league with 30 errors, and the general manager walking away from the Sox at the end of the season, only to return for 2006. Renteria went to Atlanta in 2006.

ing the bases with none out, the Red Sox choked and lost the clincher 5-3. Edgar Renteria made the last out—as he had for the Cardinals in the World Series of 2004. Chicago won on pitching, fielding and opportunistic hitting. The eventual world champs could always manufacture a run when they needed to. By contrast, Boston lost on inopportune pitching, fielding and hitting while awaiting walk-off homers.

Red Sox post-seasons can be as hectic and newsworthy as their in-seasons, and the 2005–06 hiatus was no exception. Immediately, there was another Red Sox-Yankee imbroglio. Compare the stats of Ortiz and New York third baseman Alex Rodriguez, who squared off for MVP (the stats in bold led the league):

	Ortiz	A-Rod
G	159	162
AB	601	605
R	119	**124**
H	180	**194**
HR	47	48
RBI	**148**	130
SB	1	21
AVE	.300	.321
OB%	.397	.421
SL%	.604	**.610**
TB	363	369
XBH	**88**	78

Edge to A-Rod? Perhaps. Only Rodriguez was comfortably elected because he played third base everyday while Papí rode the bench when he wasn't DHing. That decision made perfect sense if you were selecting the best all-around player. If value to team was the criterion—as it should have been—Ortiz merited MVP. And Papí's three game-winning hits to A-Rod's one don't really tell the story. He kept the Sox in games they went on to win and carried the team until Ramirez heated up. Ortiz probably would have been MVP had the Sox finished a game ahead of the Yanks.

Still more hot stove controversy settled around Fenway. On October 31, Theo Epstein resigned as general manager, dodging reporters in a gorilla suit, of all things. Once baseball's youngest general manager, Epstein, 32, had grown old in a hurry from constant squabbles with club president Larry Lucchino. In rejecting a three-year, $4.5 million contract extension, Epstein may have made a case for patiently rebuilding the club on White Sox-style pitching, speed, youth and defense over Lucchino's penchant for quick fixes. Caught in the middle was owner John (Hamlet) Henry, who couldn't bring himself to assign baseball duties to Epstein and financial matters to Lucchino.

Epstein was replaced by co-GMs Ben Cherington and Jed Hoyer, two youngsters who had worked under him. They immediately took the blame when Damon accepted a four-year, $52 million offer from the despised Yankees. Losing Damon's long hair and beard (he would trim both under a Yankee decree), not to mention limitless enthusiasm that brought smiles to the faces of aged and innocent alike, sent angst through New England even more than Pedro Martinez's departure had. The Red Sox had originally offered Damon three years at $27 million before making a final offer of four years at $40 million.

The co-GMs did make moves, however — plenty of them. Third baseman Bill Mueller and first baseman Kevin Millar were allowed to leave, and Renteria was traded to the Braves: exit three-fourths of the 2005 infield. The Sox picked up the 2003 World Series MVP pitcher Josh Beckett, second baseman Mark Loretta, third baseman Mike Lowell and first baseman J.T. Snow, a defensive specialist who was expected to share the position with Kevin Youkilis. Arroyo re-upped with the team despite potentially more enriching opportunities elsewhere. He said he just loved being a Red Sox. Team futurists looked for big things from young pitchers Jonathan Papelbon and Craig Hansen, although they were expected to begin the 2006 season in Pawtucket. Then when Epstein returned, he made a major trade with the Indians, acquiring centerfielder Coco Crisp, reliever David Riske and backup catcher Josh Bard, giving up reliever Guillermo Mota and three other players. But through it all, Ortiz remained Ortiz.

Epstein had returned "in a full-time baseball capacity" on January 19. Just what his duties would be weren't described for five days, until his superiors re-appointed him general manager, with Hoyer and Cherington assuming other titles. "This is not the same organization that Theo left," Henry said in a written statement distributed to the media. "There was enough discord then to give Theo legitimate reasons to move on." Epstein and Lucchino agreed. But a

few paragraphs later, Henry added, "The media has [sic] been in much more turmoil over the Red Sox than has been the case internally."

Epstein, who had been advising the club during his break, had his work cut out for him as spring training approached. Ramirez and Wells wanted to be traded. Meanwhile, the Sox had seven potential starting pitchers and no front-line shortstop.

Hey, they won the World Series, didn't they? And it happened in our lifetimes, didn't it? What more could a Sox fan want?

Above: *Briefly sidelined early in the 2007 season, Josh Beckett's 20-7 record was a major factor in the team's going all the way, but in 2008 injuries limited him to 12 wins.*

Below: *Centerfielder Coco Crisp here makes one of his more spectacular catches. His speed in the outfield and on the bases made him a valuable contributor to both the 2007 and 2008 seasons.*

Right: *Jonathan Papelbon, after being considered as a starter, remained the Sox's closer in both 2007 and 2008, and his stats more than justified this decision.*

The Red Sox started the 2006 season hoping that 2005 was a fluke and they'd be champions once more. They plugged the hole Renteria left with slick-fielding Alex Gonzalez from Florida and late in spring training simplified the pitching logjam by sending the loyal Arroyo to Cincinnati for reserve outfielder Wily Mo Peña.

Alas, the season resembled so many others: early promise bashed by the midseason reality of a superior Yankee team. After leading the league or being tied for the lead at the end of April, May, June and July, the Sox suffered a 9-21 August collapse that included the latest Boston Massacre, in which the Yankees swept a five-game series at Fenway by outscoring the Sox, 49-26. It was the first time they'd been blanked in a five-game series since the Indians whipped them in 1954. And for the first time since 1997, the Red Sox failed to finish second, coming in third behind Toronto with an 86-76 record.

At times, the team was a walking hospital. Pitching coach Dave Wallace nearly died from a hip infection and missed most of the season after undergoing a hip replacement. After off-season knee surgery, closer Keith Foulke had no spring training to speak of and threw just 49 2/3 innings amid back pain in his final season. Reliever Mike Timlin was disabled with a shoulder strain and never got his effectiveness back. First sidelined after knee surgery, lefthander David Wells was hit on the same knee by a line drive on May 31, ruining his

season. Crisp had a broken left index finger that limited him to 105 games of so-so performance and rookie closer Jonathan Papelbon's shoulder shut him down in September after a sterling 35 saves. Though Jason Varitek set a team record of 1,017 games caught, he needed knee surgery in early August and the team was never the same. Knuckleballer Tim Wakefield and rightfielder Trot Nixon, among others, were also disabled. Meanwhile, the discarded but healthy Arroyo went 14-11, with a 3.29 ERA, and led the National League with 35 starts and 240 1/3 innings.

Other Sox were merely disappointing. Though he went 16-11, Beckett's ERA climbed from 3.38 in 2005 to 5.01 in 2006. And Manny Ramirez was infuriating. After recording his usual 30-homer, 100-RBI season— 35 and 102, to be exact—he cited a questionable knee injury and cashiered his season after 130 games.

Oh, there were some happy times, as there always are with the Red Sox. Led by excellent fielding from Lowell (.987 percentage in 2006), Gonzalez (.985) and Loretta (.994), the team set a major-league record of 17 straight errorless games. Lowell hit .284, with 20 homers and 80 RBI. Schilling was back in form with a 15-7 record and a 3.97 ERA. And it was all Papí, all the time. David Ortiz had five game-winning hits and was an MVP candidate with 54 homers and 137 RBI. But it was emblematic of the year that even this happy panda turned grizzly when he realized that designated hitters don't get elected MVP.

"I'll tell you one thing," Ortiz told ESPN late in the season. "If I get 50 home runs and 10 more RBI [which would give him 137], that's going to be a round number that no one else in the American League will have. But they'll vote for a position player, use that as an excuse. They're talking about [the Yankees' Derek] Jeter a lot, right? He's done a great job, he's having a great season, but Jeter is not a 40-homer hitter or an RBI guy. It doesn't matter how much you've done for your ball club, the bottom line is, the guy who hits 40 home runs and knocks in 100, that's the guy you know helped your team win games.

"Don't get me wrong — he's a great player, having a great season, but he's got a lot of guys in that lineup," Ortiz continued. "Top to bottom, you've got a guy who can hurt you. Come hit in this lineup, see how good you can be."

Another Yankee-Red Sox imbroglio? Jeter didn't rise to the bait. As it happened, neither Jeter nor Ortiz was elected MVP. The award went to the Twins' Justin Morneau.

As the 2007 season approached, there was excitement aplenty around Red Sox Nation about new faces foreign and domestic, heralded rookies and veterans in their prime. Indeed, the Sox became early favorites in the AL East when they outbid the Yankees for Japanese pitcher Daisuke (Dice-K) Matsuzaka, Most Valuable Player in the 2006 World Baseball Classic and the owner of a mysterious "gyro" delivery. It cost Boston $51.1 million just to negotiate with his team, then another $52 million to sign him to a six-year contract. Boston also spent $36 million on good-hit, fair-field shortstop Julio Lugo, and $70 million for oft-injured rightfielder J.D. Drew. Combined with eight-figure annual salaries for leftfielder Manny Ramirez, DH David Ortiz, pitcher Curt Schilling and catcher Jason Varitek, the signings swelled Boston's payroll to $143 million, second only to the Yankees'.

There was some drama in spring training when Jonathan Papelbon switched from closer to the rotation and the Sox cast about desperately for a replacement. After a few sleepless nights, however, Papelbon decided he'd rather close. Going into the season, everyone expected big years from players like Ramirez, Lugo, Drew and Dice-K. So what happened?

Occasionally brilliant, Matsuzaka went 15-12 and had 201 strikeouts in 204 2/3 innings, but he also stumbled to a 4.40 ERA and his gyroball proved to be little more than a modified fadeaway. Drew batted just .270, with 11 homers and 64 RBI. Lugo batted .237, albeit with 73 RBI and 33 stolen bases. Ramirez missed 24 games with a strained muscle on the left side of his rib cage, batted .294 and dropped to 20 homers and 88 RBI.

It was just his second season in the last 10 years short of .300-30-100 production.

And yet the Sox moved into first for good on April 18, rallied from a 5-0 deficit in the ninth to beat the Orioles, 6-5, in the "Mothers' Day Miracle," and won 96 games to finish in first place, two games ahead of the Yankees. Manager Terry Francona never panicked. When rookie second baseman Dustin Pedroia was hitting .172 on May 1, the squawk radio loudmouths demanded Francona replace him with veteran Alex Cora. Francona held firm, and Pedroia righted himself to bat .317, make only six errors and stake his claim to Rookie of the Year honors. A little man (5'9") with a long swing and a rookie with a cocky attitude, "Pedey" wowed everyone when his unbelievable stop and throw preserved a no-hitter pitched by

Below: *Daisuke Matsuzaka — Dice-K — was acquired from Japan in 2007 at great cost. His 15-12 record helped the team reach the post season.*

rookie Clay Buchholz, who went 3-1 in a late-season call-up before a tired arm shut him down for the post-season.

Another surprise was reliever Hideki Okajima. A "pony to Matsuzaka's Secretariat," in the words of *Boston Globe* columnist Gordon Edes, he signed for only $2.5 million over two years and was expected to be one of those lefties brought in exclusively to face lefties. But when pitching coach John Farrell taught him a changeup-splitter known as the "Okie-Dokie," righthanders hit only .182 against him, he made the All-Star team, and finished

the season with a 2.22 ERA and 60 strike-outs in 69 innings as an ideal setup man for Papelbon. A great fan favorite, Okajima has a strange delivery in which he actually looks to his right as he releases the ball toward the plate. Supplying even more joy all around, Jon Lester made a complete recovery from lymphoma and went 4-0.

Elsewhere in the lineup, Josh Beckett had a stand-out season (20-7, 3.27 ERA), winning his 20th on September 21, when the Red Sox lead of 14 1/2 games over the Yankees had slipped to 1 1/2; Papelbon threw 12.96 strike-outs per nine-inning game and converted 37 of 40 save opportunities; third baseman Mike Lowell became unofficial team MVP when he hit .324, slugged 21 homers and batted in 121 runs; DH David Ortiz batted .441 with seven homers and 19 runs batted in over the last 16 games despite a torn meniscus in his left knee that would require off-season surgery; and first baseman Kevin Youkilis, expertly tutored by coach Luis Alicea, set an American League record with 135 error-less games covering 1,080 chances and won a Gold Glove at his new position. But for all the good news, it looked like another typical year when late-season pick-up Eric Gagné, a reliever columnists said would guarantee a flag, cost the Sox several games and the team went into a summer slump.

That's when the legend of Jacoby Ellsbury was born. An outfielder of Navajo descent who started the season at Double-A and was summoned from Triple-A Pawtucket for good on September 1, he batted .353, stole eight bases without being caught, scored from second on a wild pitch and played spectacular defense while subbing for the injured Ramirez in left. And when center-fielder Coco Crisp became expendable in a post-season batting slump, Ellsbury would have more to show.

In the American League Division Series, the Red Sox faced their country cousins from California — the Los Angeles Angels of Anaheim. Having swept them in their last two post-season engagements, the Sox saw no reason to change against a team with ailing and ineffective sluggers. Sure enough, Beckett, who bedazzled the Yankees in the 2003 World Series when he pitched for Florida, won Game 1 with a four-hit, no-walk, 4-0 whitewashing in the most dominant post-season win by a Red Sox pitcher since Luis Tiant beat Cincinnati, 6-0, in Game 1 of the 1975 Fall Classic. In Game 2, the Angels kayoed Matsuzaka with two outs in the fifth, but four Boston relievers held them hitless until Ramirez won the game, 6-3, with a three-run walk-off homer. "When you don't feel good and get hits, that's when you know you're a bad man," he said.

In Game 3, up stepped Curt Schilling, who had gone 9-8 and come within one out of a no-hitter while rebuilding himself as a finesse pitcher. Burnishing his Hall of Fame credentials in the post-season, he ended the ALDS by going seven innings and leaving with a 2-0 lead on homers by Ortiz and Ramirez before the Sox scored seven times in the eighth to win 9-1.

Next came the Indians in the American League Championship Series — and trouble. Cleveland had finished the regular season with an identical record to Boston's and had baseball's most dominant one-two punch in starters C.C. Sabathia and Fausto Carmona. After the redoubtable Beckett, Ortiz and Ramirez set them down, 10-3, in Game 1 of the ALCS, the Indians blasted the Red Sox, 13-6, in 11 innings at Fenway,

with bottomed-out Gagné taking the loss. In Game 3 at Cleveland's Jacobs Field, the Indians then blitzed Dice-K, 4-2.

The Red Sox were down, two games to one, but they'd been down three games to none in the 2004 ALCS, as Ortiz reminded his teammates when he brought them together for a players-only meeting in the post-game clubhouse. *Sports Illustrated*'s Tom Verducci reconstructed Papí's monologue:

"Listen, we're not just a good team. We're a great team... And let's go play one at a

Above: *A Gold-Glove performer at first base, Kevin Youkilis triples in Game 4 of the American League Championship Series against the Indians.*

Left: *Manny Ramirez, here hitting a homer in Game 2 of the 2007 ALCS against Cleveland, was a major factor in the Sox's World Series years.*

Above: *Mike Lowell, here batting in Game 1 of the ALCS against the Indians, went on to become the 2007 World Series MVP.*

Right: *After defeating the Indians, 11-2, the Red Sox celebrate winning the best-of-seven ALCS despite trailing three games to one.*

bration. The teams returned to Fenway Park, where Schilling gave up six hits and no walks over seven innings of a 12-2 win, and Drew climbed out of the doghouse with a first-inning grand slam. In the final game, Dice-K got through five innings with a 3-2 lead, and then Pedroia's two-run homer in the seventh and three-run double in the eighth produced an 11-2 trouncing. Papelbon danced in his underwear, with visions of being tackled by his teammates after the last out of the World Series.

The Red Sox had just won three straight elimination games by an aggregate score of 30-5 while running up a 3.60 staff ERA and a .304 team batting average in the ALCS, led by Youk's .425 hitting and Manny's four homers and 14 RBI. The Sox had trailed in only three of 63 post-season innings and outscored the Angels and Indians by a record 44 runs.

So on to the World Series against the Colorado Rockies, who had won 21 of their last 22 games. What momentum? With Pedroia hitting a leadoff homer and Beckett throwing 95-97 mph fastballs in the early innings and 75 mph curves later, the opener was never in doubt: 13-1 Sox. Colorado starter Jeff Francis needed 103 pitches to finish four innings, and his replacement Franklin Morales allowed seven runs in without finishing the fifth, a Series first, while Beckett finished his post-season with 4-0 record, a 1.30 ERA, two walks, and 35 strikeouts in 30 innings. Led by Ortiz and Ramirez, with three hits and two RBI apiece, every Sox starter got a hit or drove in a run. The

time and prove that." He started pulling up his gray road jersey. "There's a reason why you wear this uniform."

How could a team this loose be beaten? Though the Indians stopped 17-game winner Tim Wakefield, 7-3, in Game 4, no one would upend them again. In Game 5, ALCS MVP Beckett outpitched Sabathia on five hits, one walk and 11 strikeouts over eight innings, 7-1, to spoil the anticipated Cleveland cele-

Left: *American League Rookie of the Year Dustin Pedroia slides into second with a two-run, eighth-inning double in Game 3 of the 2007 World Series.*

Below: *Jacoby Ellsbury, here beating the throw to Rockies second baseman Kazuo Matsui in Game 3 of the 2007 World Series, proved a valuable end-of-season addition to the Red Sox.*

36,733 Fenway faithful were spoiled almost to the point of boredom.

Game 2 riveted them to their seats. The 40-year-old Schilling went 5 1/3 innings, allowed four singles, two walks, and a hit batsman and left with a 2-1 lead on Lowell's run-scoring double. But before Schilling could improve his post-season record to 11-2 with a 2.23 ERA and an unmatched winning percentage of .846, he needed help from what he calls "the Papa-jima show." Replacing Schilling with the tying and lead runs on base and one out in the sixth, Okajima got Garrett Atkins on a soft roller and struck out

Right: *Rejoining the team after recovering from cancer, Jon Lester was the winning pitcher in the fourth and final game of the 2007 World Series.*

Below: *The Red Sox celebrate after defeating the Rockies, 4-3, in Game 4 for a sweep of the 2007 World Series.*

Brad Hawpe. Okajima rolled through three batters in the seventh and two in the eighth, fanning four of the seven batters he faced, before Papelbon replaced him and gave up an infield single to Matt Holliday. The scouting reports said Holliday liked to run on the first pitch, and when Papelbon picked him off, the Rockies were effectively dead for the Series. Papelbon struck out two in a 1-2-3 ninth to preserve Schilling's 2-1 win.

In Game 3 Dice-K built up a 6-0 lead with 5 1/3 strong innings, even driving in two runs himself with a third-inning single. Colorado scored twice in the sixth and three times in the seventh to bring the Coors Field crowd of 49,983 to attention. Then Ellsbury got an RBI double and Pedroia a two-run double as the Sox eventually won the longest (4:19) nine-inning game in World Series history, 10-5. The two 24-year-old rookies, Pedroia and Ellsbury, went 7-for-10 for the night. Easily overlooked, shortstop Lugo made two great plays. With runners on first and second in the fifth, he ranged deep in the hole for a grounder and threw alertly to Lowell for a force at third. When the Rockies scored twice in the sixth and got two on with two out, Lugo leaped high to snare Jeff Baker's liner. "His plays might've saved the game," Lowell said.

But nothing was quite as heartening as Game 4. Fourteen months after his cancer diagnosis, Lester went 5 2/3 innings, left with a 2-0 lead and got hugs in the dugout. In a telling sequence with a runner on second in the third inning, Lester heeded scouting reports and struck out excellent but overeager hitters Troy Tulowitzki and Holliday on pitches outside the strike zone. Meanwhile, Ellsbury scored on Ortiz's first-inning single and Lowell (himself a cancer survivor) eluded a tag on a nifty slide home following Jason Varitek's fifth-inning single. Sensing triumph, Crisp put a bubble-gum balloon on Dice-K's hat while teammates cracked up.

The Red Sox added a run on a homer by Series MVP Lowell (.400, six runs, four RBI, one homer) in the seventh, but the Rockies scored once in their half before Boston pinch hitter Bobby Kielty, an Oakland reject, homered on the first pitch he saw in the eighth, running the lead to 4-1. The blast assumed outsized significance when Atkins' two-run shot off Okajima made it 4-3 with only one out in the eighth. Enter Papelbon, who hadn't been scored on in nine post-season innings. He looked around roomy Coors Field — 347 feet to left, 390 to left-center, 415 to center, 375 to right-center and 350 to right in the mile-high air — and proceeded to use it twice. First, Hawpe flied deep to center, ending the eighth. Then, with one out in the ninth, pinch hitter Jamey Carroll smacked a fat fastball and chased Ellsbury deep to left, where he caught the liner before crashing into the fence. "I was thinking, 'I'm going to get this somehow,'" he said. "If I had to climb the wall. If I had to run through the wall. But it wasn't landing."

Papelbon ended the season in more typical form by fanning pinch hitter Seth Smith on a high heater and getting mobbed by teammates.

The Red Sox had outscored the Rockies 29-10 and all their October opponents 99-46 for the greatest differential in post-season history. Everyone in the Sox clubhouse was delighted that Ellsbury, Lester, Lowell and Papelbon were final-game heroes and that Francona had become the first manager to win his first eight World Series games.

Some observers wondered if the Red Sox would become the next Evil Empire or Damn Red Sox: a team of mercenary players and fat-cat ownership spending big bucks to win one title after another. Neither label fits. The 2007 Red Sox made good use of low-priced players — Pedroia, Lester, Youkilis and Papelbon all made under $500,000 — with plans to promote more prospects from the minors.

Schilling re-signed for $8 million plus incentives in 2008, a good $5 million under his 2007 salary and well short of what he'd have made on the open market. Even as the victory caravan displaying a wild-dancing Jonathan Papelbon rolled through a 2.9-mile route in Boston on October 30, citizens and players alike pleaded for the brass to hang onto the beloved Lowell and let Yankee free agent Alex Rodriguez peddle his big bucks elsewhere.

After hosting a Halloween party for a group including teammates Doug Mirabelli and Lowell, Varitek sat on a lawn chair in the Waban neighborhood of Newton, Massachusetts, and signed baseballs, shirts, hats, a green alien's glove from a kid's costume, even a pillow case filled with candy, for 50 kids and parents, while two police cruisers arrived to direct traffic. "Waban has been good to us and respected our privacy," Tek told the *Boston Globe*. "It was a good opportunity for me to say thanks."

So when the Red Sox took the field in 2008, a better moniker was in order. How about Kindly Kingdom? Based on what hap-

Above left: *Jonathan Papelbon, in his customary high spirits, plays to the crowd during the parade through Boston to celebrate the second Red Sox World Series championship in four years.*

Above right: *David (Big Papí) Ortiz holds the World Series trophy and waves to fans during the Red Sox 2007 victory celebration in Boston.*

Above: *Manny Ramirez was running up his usual stellar numbers in 2008, but his attitude and relations with team-mates led to his being traded in mid-season.*

Right: *Mid-season 2008 acquisition Jason Bay kept the Red Sox Express running smoothly.*

pened to their veteran players, you'd have expected the team to turn nasty. The aging Schilling, whose pitching helped the team win the World Series in 2004 and 2007, was lost for the season with shoulder and biceps miseries. Beckett, twice disabled with a tired elbow and a bad back, won only 12 games. Despite an 18-3 record and a 2.90 ERA, Matsuzaka — with shoulder tendonitis — pitched only 167 2/3 innings. Ortiz injured his wrist, missed seven weeks, and saw his production fall to 23 homers and 89 RBI. After happily re-signing for less money than he'd have made on the open market, Lowell (17 homers, 73 RBI) sat out often with hand and torso muscle injuries. Varitek batted .220. And Ramirez, certain the team would exercise a one-year option rather than give him a multi-year contract, appeared to give up playing his best game.

Yet the Sox contended entertainingly and set themselves up for post-season fireworks. Now 20 months removed from his cancer diagnosis, Lester (16-6) threw a no-hitter against the Royals on May 20. Twelve days later, Ramirez hit his 500th homer at Baltimore's Camden Yards. Though Ortiz injured his wrist the same day, J.D. Drew compensated by batting .337 with 12 homers and 27 RBI in June. Then in July the club fell apart amid Manny's mouthing off. Evidenced by an at bat in which he watched three called strikes sail by, some felt he wasn't even trying. On July 30, the Sox traded Ramirez to the Dodgers in a three-way deal that landed them Pittsburgh leftfielder Jason Bay.

Before his first at bat, Bay received a standing ovation at Fenway. He promptly hit a 12th-inning triple in a Sox win and stayed so hot that headlines trumpeted "Bay State." The Red Sox went 15-7 between August 22 and September 12 using their brigade of twenty-somethings. When Lugo was hurt, Jed Lowrie played steady two-way ball. Ellsbury led the league with 50 steals, and Coco Crisp hit .283 and didn't complain about his utility role. The team's steadiest players were Kevin Youkilis and Dustin Pedroia. Youk hit .312, with 29 homers and 115 RBI while manning first and occasionally third. Pedroia was simply out-of-sight. The 2007 Rookie of the Year, he earned the 2008 Most Valuable Player award by hitting .326; stealing 20 bases; leading the league with 118 runs, 54 doubles and 213 hits; and contributing excellent production for a second baseman with 17 homers and 83 RBI. The little park rat got another Gold Glove, too.

The Sox finished as 95-67 wild card winners to make the post season for the fifth time in six years. Up next: the Los Angeles Angels, who copped the league's best record (100-62), with Frankie (K-Rod) Rodriguez,

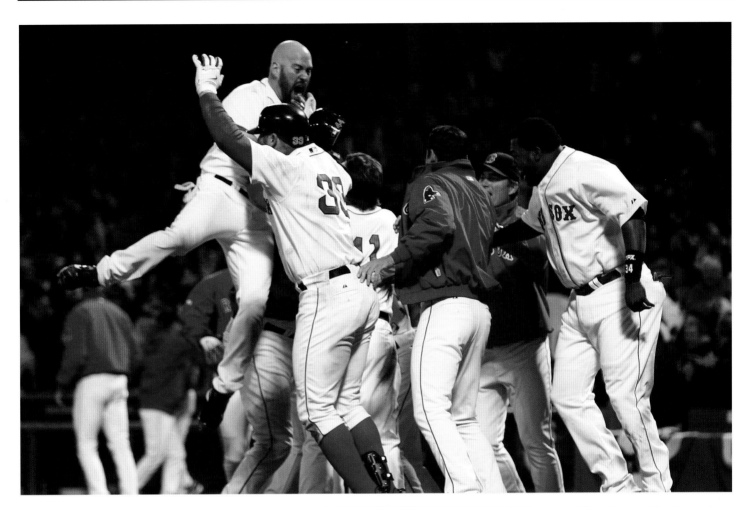

(major-league record 62 saves), Joe Saunders (17-7, 3.41 ERA) and Ervin Santana (16-7, 3.49) compensating for an unusually anemic (765 runs) offense.

The Red Sox literally walked off with the ALDS. After the redoubtable Lester retired LA, 4-1, in the Angel Stadium opener, the Red Sox won Game 2, 7-5, on Drew's two-run homer off K-Rod in the ninth. Returning home with a 2-0 lead in a best-of-five series, Boston could afford to be complacent. So what if they lost Game 3, 5-4, in 12 innings and the Angels ended an 11-game post-season losing streak to the Red Sox? Boston took Game 4, 3-2, amid much drama in the ninth. With the score 2-2, LA's Erick Aybar failed to get down a suicide squeeze that probably would have scored Reggie Willits from third. Varitek ran him down and made a diving tag. With one out in the Red Sox ninth, Bay doubled. An out later, Lowrie's walk-off single scored Bay to end the ALDS. Teammates greeted Bay (7-for-17, 2 homers, 5 RBI) at the plate, then rushed to engulf kid shortstop Lowrie at first.

There were still Joe Maddon's Rays to contend with if the Red Sox hoped to be the 21st century's first repeat champions. Tampa Bay had made short work of the White Sox in a four-game ALDS and looked ready to polish off the Red Sox as well. To be sure, the Sox looked unbeatable in Game 1 at indoor, funereal Tropicana

Above: *The Sox, celebrating their 2008 ALDS victory over the LA Angels, showed they could beat any team but the Tampa Bay Rays this year.*

Left: *Catcher and team captain Jason Varitek led the club in the field in 2008 but slumped to .220.*

Above: *Jed Lowrie, brought up from Pawtucket when Julio Lugo was hurt in 2008, played excellent short-stop and drove in 46 runs over 81 games.*

Right: *Dice-K, here conferring with Varitek, showed his mettle with men on base and improved to 18-3 in 2008.*

Field, when Dice-K threw six no-hit innings and won, 2-0, on Lowrie's sac fly in the fifth and Youk's RBI double in the eighth. The next day, though, the Rays won a 5-hour, 27-minute, 11-inning marathon, 9-8, when B.J. Upton's sac fly off Mike Timlin scored Fernando Perez. The teams had traded homers — an LCS record seven of them — while the lead changed hands three times.

The scene shifted to Fenway Park and grew downright embarrassing for the hosts. Matt Garza outpitched Lester, 9-1, in Game 3, and Andy Sonnanstine humiliated Tim Wakefield in a 13-4 blowout that put the Red Sox one loss from death's door. You could excuse fans for leaving Fenway with the Rays leading Game 5, 7-0, halfway through the seventh.

Shame on them! With Grant Balfour in relief of Scott Kazmir, Lowrie led off with a double. Two outs later, Crisp singled Lowrie to third and Pedroia went eight pitches into his at bat before singling Lowrie home. The Rays still led, 7-1, but they were getting careless. Balfour threw one into Ortiz's wheelhouse — down and in — and he homered to make it 7-4. Dan Wheeler got the Rays out of the inning.

In the eighth, closer Papelbon, who had reported for emergency duty in the seventh, got the Rays in order. Then Wheeler walked

Left: Kevin Youkilis ran up his best numbers in 2008 — 29 HR, 115 RBI and a .312 BA — while alternating between first and third.

Below: Dustin Pedroia won American League MVP honors in 2008 as well as another Gold Glove for his play around second base.

Bay on four pitches and surrendered a two-run homer to Drew. It was now 7-6, and no one was leaving. Sean Casey and Lowrie made outs, but Mark Kotsay doubled. Whereupon Crisp fouled one pitch after another off the fat part of his bat — always a good sign — before singling on the 10th pitch to tie the game.

Fenway had morphed into the Eagles song "Witchy Woman," with echoed voices, dancing shadows, restless spirits filling the air. Justin Masterson got through the top of the ninth. In the bottom, J.P. Howell retired Pedroia on a grounder, struck out Ortiz and appeared to get his team into extra innings when third baseman Evan Longoria made a nice backhand stop of Youk's tricky bouncer. But Longoria bounced his throw, sending Youk to second. Howell walked Bay to reach Drew. Are you kidding? J.D. Drew is a professional hitter; he carries his bat around like a hunter with his rifle. Drew singled over the drawn-in outfield, and the Red Sox won, 8-7.

It was the second greatest comeback in post-season history, topped only by the 1929 Philadelphia Athletics, who rebounded from an 8-0 deficit to beat the Cubs, 10-8, in the World Series. It was also Boston's eighth consecutive win in a post-season elimination game, dating back to four in 2004 and three in 2007. Surely, the Red Sox were now headed for another Fall Classic, even if they had to stop by Maddon's mausoleum for two games on the way. As if on cue, Beckett beat Jamie Shields, 4-2, in Game 6. Alas,

Garza beat Lester, 3-1, in the finale. You had to say, hats off to the Rays, a superior team all season.

Fret not, Red Sox fans. Just think what a healthy Olde Towne Team could do in 2009.

Red Sox Achievements

YEAR-BY-YEAR RED SOX STANDINGS

Year	Pos.	Record	Games Behind	Manager	Year	Pos.	Record	Games Behind	Manager
1901	2	79-57	4	Collins	1956	4	84-70	13	Higgins
1902	3	77-60	6½	Collins	1957	3	82-72	16	Higgins
1903	1	91-47	+14½	Collins	1958	3	79-75	13	Higgins
1904	1	95-59	+1½	Collins	1959	5	75-79	19	Higgins/Jurges
1905	4	78-74	16	Collins	1960	7	65-89	32	Jurges/Higgins
1906	8	49-105	45½	Collins/Stahl	1961	6	76-86	33	Higgins
1907	7	59-90	32½	Huff/Unglaub/	1962	8	76-84	19	Higgins
				McGuire	1963	7	76-85	28	Pesky
1908	5	75-79	15½	McGuire/Lake	1964	8	72-90	27	Pesky/Herman
1909	3	88-63	9½	Lake	1965	9	62-100	40	Herman
1910	4	81-72	22½	Donovan	1966	9	72-90	26	Herman/Runnels
					1967	1	92-70	+1	Williams
1911	5	78-75	24	Donovan	1968	4	86-76	17	Williams
1912	1	105-47	+14	Stahl	1969	3	87-75	22	Williams/Popowski
1913	4	79-71	15½	Stahl/Carrigan	1970	3	87-75	21	Kasko
1914	2	91-62	8½	Carrigan	1971	3	85-77	18	Kasko
1915	1	101-50	+2½	Carrigan	1972	2	85-70	½	Kasko
1916	1	91-63	+2	Carrigan	1973	2	89-73	8	Kasko
1917	2	90-62	9	Barry	1974	3	84-78	7	Johnson
1918	1	75-51	+1½	Barrow	1975	1	95-65	+4 ½	Johnson
1919	6	66-71	20½	Barrow	1976	3	83-79	15 ½	Johnson/Zimmer
1920	5	72-81	25½	Barrow	1977	2	97-64	2 ½	Zimmer
1921	5	75-79	23½	Duffy	1978	2	99-64	1	Zimmer
1922	8	61-93	33	Duffy	1979	3	91-69	11 ½	Zimmer
1923	8	61-91	37	Chance	1980	4	83-77	19	Zimmer/Pesky
1924	7	67-87	25	Fohl	1981	5/2	59-49	x	Houk
1925	8	47-105	49½	Fohl	1982	3	89-73	6	Houk
1926	8	46-107	44½	Fohl	1983	6	78-84	20	Houk
1927	8	51-103	59	Carrigan	1984	4	86-76	18	Houk
1928	8	57-96	43½	Carrigan	1985	5	81-81	18 ½	McNamara
1929	8	58-96	48	Carrigan	1986	1	95-66	+15 ½	McNamara
1930	8	52-102	50	Wagner	1987	5	78-84	20	McNamara
1931	6	62-90	45	Collins	1988	1	89-73	+1	McNamara/Morgan
1932	8	43-111	64	Collins/McManus	1989	3	83-79	6	Morgan
1933	7	63-86	34½	McManus	1990	1	88-74	+2	Morgan
1934	4	76-76	24	Harris	1991	2	84-78	7	Morgan
1935	4	78-75	16	Cronin	1992	7	73-89	23	Hobson
1936	6	74-80	28½	Cronin	1993	5	80-82	15	Hobson
1937	5	80-72	21	Cronin	1994	4	54-61#	17	Hobson
1938	2	88-61	9½	Cronin	1995	1	86-58	+7	Kennedy
1939	2	89-62	17	Cronin	1996	3	85-77	7	Kennedy
1940	4	82-72	8	Cronin	1997	4	78-84	20	Williams
1941	2	84-70	17	Cronin	1998	2*	92-70	22	Williams
1942	2	93-59	9	Cronin	1999	2*	94-68	4	Williams
1943	7	68-84	29	Cronin	2000	2	85-77	2	Williams
1944	4	77-77	12	Cronin	2001	2	82-79	13	Kerrigan
1945	7	71-83	17½	Cronin	2002	2	93-69	10	Little
1946	1	104-50	+12	Cronin	2003	2*	95-67	6	Little
1947	3	83-71	14	Cronin	2004	2*	98-64	3	Francona
1948	2	96-59	1	McCarthy	2005	1*	95-67	0	Francona
1949	2	96-58	1	McCarthy	2006	3	86-76	11	Francona
1950	3	94-60	4	McCarthy/O'Neill	2007	1	96-66	0	Francona
1951	3	87-67	11	O'Neill	2008	2	95-67	2	Francona
1952	6	76-78	19	Boudreau					
1953	4	84-69	16	Boudreau					
1954	4	69-85	42	Boudreau	# = Strike-shortened season				
1955	4	84-70	12	Higgins	* = Wildcard				

RED SOX POST-SEASON RECORD

Playoffs

Year	Opponent	Win-Loss
Division		
1995	Cleveland	0-3
1998	Cleveland	1-3
1999	Cleveland	3-2
2003	Oakland	3-2
2004	Anaheim	3-0
2005	Chicago	0-3
2007	Los Angeles	3-0
2008	Los Angeles	3-1
League		
1948	Cleveland	0-1
1975	Oakland	3-0
1978	New York	0-1
1986	California	4-3
1988	Oakland	0-4
1990	Oakland	0-4
1999	Yankees	1-4
2003	Yankees	3-4
2004	Yankees	4-3
2007	Cleveland	4-3
2008	Tampa Bay Rays	3-4
World Series		
1903	Pittsburgh	5-3
1912	New York	*4-3-1
1915	Phillies	4-1
1916	Dodgers	4-1
1918	Cubs	4-2
1946	Cardinals	3-4
1967	Cardinals	3-4
1975	Reds	3-4
1986	Mets	3-4
2004	Cardinals	4-0
2007	Rockies	4-0

* = Tie game called for darkness

ALL-TIME RED SOX CAREER BATTING LEADERS

Games Played	Carl Yastrzemski	3,308
At Bats	Carl Yastrzemski	11,988
Hits	Carl Yastrzemski	3,419
Batting Average	Ted Williams	.344
Home Runs	Ted Williams	521
Runs Scored	Carl Yastrzemski	1,816
Runs Batted In	Carl Yastrzemski	1,844
Strikeouts	Carl Yastrzemski	1,393
Stolen Bases	Harry Hooper	300

ALL-TIME RED SOX CAREER PITCHING LEADERS

Innings Pitched	Cy Young	2,728.1
Wins	Cy Young	192
	Roger Clemens	192
Losses	Cy Young	112
Winning %	Pedro Martinez	.760
ERA	Smokey Joe Wood	1.96
Strikeouts	Roger Clemens	2,590
Game Appearances	Bob Stanley	637
Shutouts	Cy Young	38
	Roger Clemens	38
No-Hitters	Cy Young	2
	Dutch Leonard	2
Perfect Games	Cy Young	1
	Ernie Shore	1
Saves	Bob Stanley	132

HALL OF FAMERS

Name	Position	Year Elected
Babe Ruth	P, OF	1936
Tris Speaker	OF	1937
Cy Young	P	1937
Jimmy Collins	3B	1945
Lefty Grove	P	1947
Herb Pennock	P	1948
Jimmie Foxx	1B	1951
Joe Cronin	SS	1956
Ted Williams	OF	1966
Red Ruffing	P	1967
Harry Hooper	OF	1971
George Kell	3B	1983
Luis Aparicio	SS	1984
Rick Ferrell	C	1984
Bobby Doerr	2B	1986
Carl Yastrzemski	OF, 1B	1989
Carlton Fisk	C	2000
Dennis Eckersley	P	2004
Wade Boggs	3B	2005

SINGLE-SEASON RED SOX BATTING RECORDS

Batting Average (500 ABs)	Ted Williams	.406	1941
Hits	Wade Boggs	240	1985
Home Runs	Jimmie Foxx	50	1938
Runs Batted In	Jimmie Foxx	175	1938
Singles	Wade Boggs	187	1985
Doubles	Earl Webb	67	1931
Triples	Tris Speaker	22	1913
Slugging %	Ted Williams	.735	1941
Strikeouts	Butch Hobson	162	1977
Hitting Streak	Dom DiMaggio	34	1949
Grand Slams	Babe Ruth	4	1919

SINGLE-SEASON RED SOX PITCHING RECORDS

Wins	Smokey Joe Wood	34	1912
Losses	Charles Ruffing	25	1928
ERA (150 Innings)	Dutch Leonard	1.00	1914
Winning % (10 Decisions)	Bob Stanley	.882	1978
Strikeouts	Roger Clemens	291	1988
Saves	Tom Gordon	46	1998
Innings Pitched	Cy Young	384.2	1902
Game Appearances	Greg Harris	80	1993
Shutouts	Cy Young	10	1904
	Joe Wood	10	1912